T0170740

Revolution & Aftermath

Forging a New Strategy toward
IRAN

*The Hoover Institution gratefully acknowledges
the following individuals and foundations
for their significant support of the*

HERBERT AND JANE DWIGHT WORKING GROUP
ON ISLAMISM AND THE INTERNATIONAL ORDER:

Herbert and Jane Dwight

Donald and Joan Beall
   Beall Family Foundation

S.D. Bechtel, Jr. Foundation

Lynde and Harry Bradley Foundation

Stephen and Susan Brown

Lakeside Foundation

Nancy Doyle, M.D.

HERBERT AND JANE DWIGHT WORKING GROUP ON ISLAMISM AND THE INTERNATIONAL ORDER

Revolution & Aftermath

Forging a New Strategy toward

IRAN

Eric Edelman *and* Ray Takeyh

HOOVER INSTITUTION PRESS
Stanford University | *Stanford, California*

With its eminent scholars and world-renowned library and archives, the Hoover Institution seeks to improve the human condition by advancing ideas that promote economic opportunity and prosperity, while securing and safeguarding peace for America and all mankind. The views expressed in its publications are entirely those of the authors and do not necessarily reflect the views of the staff, officers, or Board of Overseers of the Hoover Institution.

www.hoover.org

Hoover Institution Press Publication No. 689
Hoover Institution at Leland Stanford Junior University,
Stanford, California 94305-6003

Copyright © 2018 by the Board of Trustees of the
    Leland Stanford Junior University
All rights reserved. No part of this publication may be reproduced,
stored in a retrieval system, or transmitted in any form or by any means,
electronic, mechanical, photocopying, recording, or otherwise, without
written permission of the publisher and copyright holders.

For permission to reuse material from *Revolution and Aftermath: Forging a New Strategy toward Iran*, by Eric Edelman and Ray Takeyh, ISBN 978-0-8179-2154-5, please access www.copyright.com or contact the Copyright Clearance Center, Inc. (CCC), 222 Rosewood Drive, Danvers, MA 01923, (978) 750-8400. CCC is a not-for-profit organization that provides licenses and registration for a variety of uses.

Hoover Institution Press assumes no responsibility for the persistence or accuracy of URLs for external or third-party Internet websites referred to in this publication, and does not guarantee that any content on such websites is, or will remain, accurate or appropriate.

First printing 2018
25 24 23 22 21 20 19 18   9 8 7 6 5 4 3 2 1

Manufactured in the United States of America

The paper used in this publication meets the minimum requirements of the American National Standard for Information Sciences—Permanence of Paper for Printed Library Materials, ANSI/NISO Z39.48-1992. ♾

Cataloging-in-Publication Data is available from the Library of Congress.
ISBN 978-0-8179-2154-5 (cloth : alk. paper)
ISBN 978-0-8179-2156-9 (EPUB)
ISBN 978-0-8179-2157-6 (Mobipocket)
ISBN 978-0-8179-2158-3 (PDF)

*Eric Edelman dedicates
this effort to the memories of
Alexander and Milton Edelman.*

*Ray Takeyh dedicates this work
to Alex and Nick.*

CONTENTS

ACKNOWLEDGMENTS

Eric Edelman would like to thank his colleagues Tom Mahnken, Hal Brands, and Whitney Morgan McNamara for stimulating discussions on the role of Iran in US grand strategy past and present, and to Roger Hertog whose generous support over many years has permitted deeper study of US-Iranian relations than would otherwise have been possible.

Ray Takeyh wishes to acknowledge Richard Haass and James Lindsay of the Council on Foreign Relations for providing him a great intellectual environment.

Both authors would like to thank Charles Hill and Russell Berman for suggesting that they take up this topic.

PREFACE

THIS EXTENDED ESSAY IS THE WORK OF TWO AUTHORS—ONE primarily a former government practitioner with a background as a historian of American diplomatic history and the other a longtime student of Iran with recent government experience. They hope to illuminate a subject which has been surrounded by no shortage of heated polemics in recent years but which has generally lacked critical historical context. Iran is, and will likely remain, a major strategic challenge for the Trump administration and for US policy-makers more broadly over the next decade and beyond. Developing an approach to containing Iran's hegemonic regional ambitions is an urgent requirement for the new national security team in Washington. However, unless senior US officials can disenthrall themselves from some of the persistent myths that have attended American-Iranian relations and grasp the lessons of almost forty years of confrontation with Iran's revolutionary regime, it is unlikely that they will be able to successfully come to grips with the enormous challenge at hand.

Since the Iranian revolution and the subsequent hostage crisis, Americans have consistently seen the Islamic Republic as one of the United States' leading international adversaries. Current polling puts Iran only slightly behind North Korea, whose young leader's brandishing of nuclear weapons has dominated the 24/7 American news cycle since President

Trump's inauguration. Iranian leaders, for their part, continue to identify the United States as the Great Satan and the leader of international arrogance. They have employed a number of asymmetric tools to diminish US standing in the world and reduce America's military presence in the region.

The profound disruption and dislocation occasioned by the Islamic Revolution set off historical forces that overturned the basic postulates of US post-World War II policy in the region, replacing secular radicalism with religiously based political movements as the driving ideological force in the Middle East and giving new prominence to sectarian divisions whose salience has only increased in recent years. Not all of the maladies that afflict the Near East are traceable to the events of 1979. But much of the extraordinary violence and mayhem that now seem to dominate this pivotal geopolitical space owe their origins to the overthrow of the shah and the installation of the Islamic Republic.

As this essay argues, Iran had played an underappreciated role in US grand strategy since the end of World War II. It had been a cause of the initial rupture between the United States and the Soviet Union, a battleground for influence between Russia and the West, a testing ground for various US policies in the Third World, and a key pillar of US security policy in the increasingly vital Gulf region. In the 1940s, the United States provided political support for countries resisting Soviet pressures; in the 1950s Iran became the Eisenhower administration's test case for the use of covert action; in the 1960s the Kennedy-Johnson administration tried out its theories of agrarian reform and modernization with the shah's "White

Revolution"; and in the 1970s, the Nixon doctrine's main beneficiary was Iran. The shock of the revolution, the seizure of
US diplomats as hostages, and the emergence of Iranian-
sponsored terrorist proxies in Lebanon was a disorienting
experience for US policy-makers who had become accustomed
to seeing the shah as an island of stability in a turbulent part of
the globe. It was only natural, perhaps, that they would seek a
return to something that looked like the status quo ante.

Beginning in the Carter administration, US policy-makers
systematically misread the political dynamics inside Iran. They
began the search for what former secretary of defense Robert
Gates termed "the elusive Iranian moderates" who would
polish the rough edges off the Iranian revolution and reengage
with the United States on the basis of realpolitik considerations
of Iran's position vis-à-vis its Arab neighbors and the Soviet
Union/Russia (with whom the country had long had an antago-
nistic relationship).[1] There was a persistent failure to appreciate
the uniqueness of Iran's status as a revolutionary state committed to upending not just the regional distribution of power but
the global correlation of forces as well.

American officials persistently failed to take seriously the
underlying fact of Ayatollah Ruhollah Khomeini's successful
transformation of fundamental Shiite political values. From a
tradition that had previously counseled quietism and acceptance of the existing political authorities, Khomeini wrought a
political culture committed to the notion that everything is
political and that the only acceptable form of government
under Islam was the government of God, implemented by the
most authoritative jurist in the land.

Moreover, Americans missed the genius of the mixed constitution that Khomeini contrived out of the initial chaos of the
revolution. A constitutional theocracy with a veneer of popular
sovereignty and an electoral system that functioned as a safety
valve for popular discontent turned out to be remarkably
durable. This durability, which went against the expectations of
experts and officials, was reinforced by the uncanny ability of
the regime to renew itself with a second generation of revolutionary believers who had been forged in the crucible of the
Iran-Iraq War. The regime also had a tripod of support in the
form of the Iranian Revolutionary Guards, the intelligence services, and paramilitary thugs who could be counted on to impose
the regime's will on dissenters who might take to the streets.

Americans also failed to understand that the regime drew
sustenance from a foreign policy that was explicitly fashioned
to uphold and reinforce the regime's ideological identity. This
foreign policy was based on Khomeini's insight that the vitality
of Islamism at home depended on the successful export of Islam
abroad. Essentially, Khomeini did not believe in Islamism in
one country: only a permanent revolution spreading throughout the region could survive in the long run. This understanding gave early rise to Iran's involvement in Lebanon and
subversion in the Gulf. It remains today as the underpinning of
Iran's bid for hegemony in the region.

Despite the suspicion and animosity engendered by the
1979–81 hostage crisis, along with Iranian-inspired terrorist
attacks against Americans for three decades (including the
bombings of the Marine barracks in Beirut and the Air Force
apartment building in Khobar Towers), there has been no

shortage of diplomatic engagement between the United States and the Islamic Republic. Ranging from President Jimmy Carter's effort to free the American diplomats held hostage for 444 days, to President Reagan's efforts to liberate Americans abducted by Iranian proxies in Lebanon, and including efforts by George W. Bush and Barack Obama to negotiate limitations to Iran's pursuit of nuclear weapons capability, these diplomatic efforts have revealed strikingly similar patterns of negotiating behavior and an Iranian operational code that bears study.

Americans have persistently operated on a flawed reading of Iran's domestic politics, one that has hamstrung and disabled American diplomacy and yielded three important lessons. First, Americans have tended to see Iran as a collection of factions that the United States can manipulate to achieve its ends in negotiations. Factionalism has certainly existed, but multiple US negotiating efforts have foundered on America's crippling inability to decode the fault lines in ways that make a difference. In fact, on the core issues of Iran's pursuit of regional hegemony and nuclear weapons capability, Iranian leaders have forged a broad consensus, although tactical differences may continue to exist. Moreover, the excessive focus on factionalism has frequently led Americans to turn a blind eye to Iran's transgressions against human rights at home and flagrant violations of international law in its acts of subversion and support for terrorism.

Second, Americans have frequently worried that threats of force would undercut their efforts to empower the moderates who, purportedly, would be more amenable to negotiated solutions on terms acceptable to the United States. In fact, Iran has repeatedly shown itself susceptible to coercive threats about the possible use of force. The hostage crisis itself, for example, was resolved, at least in part, because Iran feared that President Ronald Reagan might use force to resolve it. The Clinton administration's quiet threats after Khobar Towers led to a stand-down of Iranian intelligence efforts for some time. The American-led military operations in Afghanistan and Iraq, as well as the exposure of Libya's nuclear program, led the Iranians to temporarily freeze some of the militarization activities in their own nuclear program.

Finally, for the life of the Islamic regime, American presidents have routinely nursed the vain hope that offers of dialogue, negotiations, and a resumption of something like normal relations would facilitate Iran becoming a responsible stakeholder in the Middle East, content to reach a modus vivendi with its neighbors. None of them were able to face up to the inconvenient truth that Iran is a revolutionary state whose identity is defined by its hostility to the Great Satan and everything it represents in international affairs.

Iran is one of several challenges facing US policy-makers, but it is the key challenge in the broader Middle East. Even the fight against jihadists is related to the Iranian search for mastery in the region. Although Iran does not represent the kind of existential threat that the Soviet Union presented during the Cold War, the current task of US policy vis-à-vis Iran is not dissimilar to the task that faced Reagan upon entering office in 1981. The issue is less the renegotiation of a badly flawed arms control agreement in the form of the Joint Comprehensive Plan of Action (JCPOA) and more the development of a comprehensive strategy and policy to contain and ultimately undermine the Islamic Republic.

Economic sanctions are the fundamental basis of any reasonable strategy for pressuring Iran. The power of sanctions was demonstrated in the late Bush and early Obama years, when the Iranian economy began to shrink and was brought to the point of collapse. Starving the regime of resources will both undermine the domestic patronage networks that support the regime at home and limit its ability to wreak havoc beyond Iran's borders.

Pushing back against Iranian adventurism in the region requires strengthening America's traditional alliances with both Israel and key Sunni Arab states. In fact, it will require a willingness to take advantage of the novel strategic circumstances that have promoted quiet, sub-rosa cooperation between Israel and both the Kingdom of Saudi Arabia and the United Arab Emirates (UAE), as well as with Egypt and Jordan. The potential for a major strategic realignment of the region is real, but it will require careful and sustained leadership. Recent efforts to repair the frayed relationships left in the wake of the Obama administration's outreach to Iran are again a good first step. But the violent civil war in Yemen and the recent dustup between Saudi Arabia and the UAE and Qatar are reminders that this will be no easy task. A robust diplomatic platform will be necessary for success.

Weakening Iran's economy and raising the costs of the Islamic Republic's overseas adventurism are important prerequisites of US strategy, but they must be supplemented by unremitting support to the dissenters inside Iran who are demanding that the regime respect basic human rights. This is not merely an indulgence of traditional American idealism, but a crucial step toward undermining the Iranian regime's moral authority and political legitimacy in the region. The Iranian people have several times in the past hundred years taken their political fate into their own hands. Until they do it again and eliminate the dictatorship of clerics, the United States will be fated to a long twilight struggle with the mullahs' regime.

1

The Permanent Revolution?

It is often claimed that every revolution contains the seeds of its own destruction. After a spasm of radical overreach, the revolutionaries yield to the temptations of pragmatism. The need to actually run a government and address domestic concerns eventually causes them to come to terms with the international order. Like the French Revolution, all subsequent regimes have their Thermidorian Reaction. No nation can live on ideology alone, and the imperative of staying in power forces erstwhile radicals to soften their edges. The twentieth-century Chinese experience tends to define our view of how modern revolutionary regimes evolve. After decades of agitating against the prevailing order, Mao Zedong's successors accepted its legitimacy and abandoned communism for a more workable capitalist system. The lure of commerce proved too tempting, as the Chinese revolutionaries soon transformed themselves into savvy businessmen. China is not alone in its journey, as Vietnam and even Cuba are mending their ways. Revolutionaries can either continue to celebrate their ideals or maintain power. They cannot do both.

Why has Iran defied this pattern? In the next chapter, we shall examine how foreign policy has been used systematically to sustain the revolution at home. In this chapter, however, the focus will be on the basic domestic arrangements that tether the Islamic Republic firmly to its founding beliefs. It is becoming increasingly clear that Ayatollah Khomeini was the most successful revolutionary of the twentieth century. While Vladimir Lenin, Mao Zedong, and Ho Chi Minh would no longer recognize the polities that they attempted to transform with revolutions, Khomeini's ideas continue to animate the regime he left behind. Through an ideology that he concocted, institutions that he created, and an elite that he molded, Khomeini remains a central figure in Iran nearly three decades after his death.

The endurance of Khomeini's message belies the notion of him as a stern mullah professing a retrogressive ideology. The Imam, as his followers would call him, forged his own path and articulated a distinct set of ideas that integrated Islamic principles, populist slogans, and Persian nationalist themes into a seamless narrative. The Islamic Republic was to defend Iran's national rights and prevent the exploitation of its resources by foreigners that had been so commonplace throughout its history. Khomeini may have been ignorant of economics, but the revolution was as much about coin as God. The new regime committed itself to providing cradle-to-grave social services to the poor and the peasantry. At times this smacked of class warfare, as the regime expropriated the property of the wealthy and dispersed it to the theocracy's lower-class constituents.

Subsidies and material rewards would become an important pillar of the legitimacy of the regime, much to its eventual chagrin. The government that Khomeini left behind proved to be incapable of producing a vibrant economy and unable to relieve itself of onerous subsidies, thereby laying the foundation of an insoluble dilemma for its successors.

The flirtation with progressive concepts of economic redistribution ought not to be confused with any inclination by Khomeini to accept a system of government based on anything but an inflexible adherence to his interpretation of Islam. In his most influential book, *The Islamic Government*, Khomeini radically departed from the prevailing Shiite traditions of political disengagement. His concept of *velayat-e faqih* (guardianship of the jurist) called for direct assumption of power by the clergy. After all, the Prophet of Islam was not just a spiritual guide but also an administrator, a dispenser of justice, and a political figure. Given the need to conform the social order to religious injunctions, the clergy must rule, as they are most knowledgeable in matters of religious law. Khomeini disdained those who urged that the clergy retreat to the mosque and leave politics to the professionals. In Iran, the mullahs dispensed with the seminaries for the more exhilarating task of creating and administering a religious state.

In fact, it is precisely reliance on religion that sets apart Khomeini's revolutionary experiment from his twentieth-century counterparts. The Islamic Republic is different from its radical peers as the ideology of the state is its religion. To be sure, this is a politicized and radicalized variation of Shiite Islam and Khomeini's experiment does contradict normative

Shiite political ideas that have evolved over centuries. Still, religion is the official dogma. A dedicated core of supporters remained loyal to this ideology, determined to perpetuate it long after Khomeini himself disappeared from the scene. Revolutionary regimes have usually collapsed when their once-ardent supporters abandoned their faith. Mikhail Gorbachev and his cohort of reformers ultimately had to accept the fact that Lenin's patrimony had failed them and that his brainchild had to be disposed of in the dustbin of history. Mao's loyalists pay tribute to him at official ceremonies and then rule the state by capitalist precepts that he would find appalling. And the Vietnamese rulers are too busy attracting Western tourists and hosting American presidents to create a Marxist utopia in Southeast Asia. It is, after all, easy to be an ex-Marxist, as this is merely a sign of intellectual maturity. But how easy is it to become an ex-Shiite? In the former case, it is mere political defection; in the latter, it is apostasy. Although the Islamic Republic has become unpopular over the years, for a small but fervent segment of the population it is still an important experiment of realizing God's will on earth. And it is this sector of society that continues to produce leaders who are determined to return to the "roots of the revolution" and that provides a pool of enforcers who are willing to shed blood in the name of God.

Khomeini's concept of Islamic government may have been for the people, but it certainly was not meant to be democratic. The Imam created a set of institutions that not only ensured clerical political hegemony but also protected his revolution's values from the inevitable forces of change. The Islamic Republic's constitution enshrined the unprecedented theory of *velayat-e faqih*, whereby a supreme leader would oversee all national affairs. The office designated for Khomeini himself had virtually unlimited responsibility and was empowered to command the armed forces and the newly created Revolutionary Guards, dismiss any elected official, countermand parliamentary legislation, and declare war and peace. The new office was subject to neither elections nor the scrutiny of the larger public. Islamic law was to displace the existing legal codes, circumscribing individual rights and prerogatives. A Guardian Council, composed mainly of clerics, was to vet all legislation, ensuring its conformity with Islamic strictures. All candidates for public office had to submit their credentials to the Guardian Council for approval. Yet another clerical body, the Assembly of Experts, would be responsible for choosing the next supreme leader. The constitutional arrangements guaranteed that Khomeini's reinterpretation of Shiism would remain the ideology of the state and that only those devoted to his vision would command state institutions.

Throughout his life, Khomeini despised democratic norms and rarely made references to a republic. For him, Iran was not an Islamic republic but an Islamic state. He firmly believed that laws should be derived from Koranic sources as applied to contemporary conditions by a clerical elite. Thus, traditional democratic institutions and practices such as assemblies, the right to vote, and referenda had no place in his political imagination. He insisted that people had to be guided by the righteous and the public had to submit to the authority of the clerical class. Unlike many of his younger disciples, Khomeini saw limited utility even in the façade of republicanism. Khomeini's concept of proper governance was a religious autocracy that could not be reconciled with pluralistic concepts.

Had Khomeini remained faithful to his concept of absolutist rule, his religious state may not have endured. The genius of the Islamic Republic is that it contains within its autocratic structure elected institutions that have little power but still provide the public with the means for expressing its grievances. In the absence of such a safety valve, however superficial, the state would have confronted even more protests than it has already. The inclusion of provisions for electoral politics in the constitution stemmed from the nature of the revolutionary coalition that overthrew the shah and seized power in 1979. Khomeini and his disciples may have led the revolt, but the support and participation of many liberals and secularists were critical to its success. The revolution called for creating a state that would be religious in its character but democratic in its procedures. This would prove an impossible task. A state can draw its legitimacy from either elections or religious dogma. The Islamic Republic bears all the hallmarks of a dictatorship, but maintains a thin veneer of collective action.

The Islamic Republic does have an elected president, a parliament, and local councils. These offices may be subordinated to the clerical bodies, but they are not entirely insignificant. The office of the president appoints the heads of government ministries, administers the bureaucracy, and frequently represents Iran at international fora. Although all of the candidates for office must be approved by the Guardian Council, the Islamic Republic has nonetheless featured a diverse collection of presidents. During the past three decades, the presidency has changed hands from a reformer with a genuine desire to foster change to an unreconstructed reactionary and finally to a cunning pragmatist. The fact that the Iranian people can have a say in who becomes president and which candidates become members of the parliament gives them the ability to express their grievances in an orderly manner. An Iran that has gone from the fiery Mahmoud Ahmadinejad to the more temperate Hassan Rouhani gives members of the public the hope that they can have a voice in national deliberations. This hope may be a delusion, and the elections have hardly affected the essential distribution of power. But they have fostered the impression that the citizenry is not a mere bystander in the game of clerical politics.

To become a revolutionary and risk one's life for a cause that seems distant, if not improbable, is one of the most crucial decisions any citizen will make. All social protest movements battle against great odds at their outset and history has shown that most revolutions fail. At times, desperate masses have seen little choice but to revolt. They did so in Iran when the shah's monarchy offered them no avenue for expressing their legitimate grievances other than protests in the streets. The Islamic Republic does offer the public the opportunity to participate on the national scene, but it is an opportunity hemmed in on all sides by clerical fiat. Still, when an average citizen is faced with a choice of rebelling against a vicious system or casting a ballot that will have a limited impact, he will probably opt for the latter. The elected institutions of Iran will not govern the theocracy, but they do provide it with an important safety valve.

All this is not to suggest that the clerical oligarchs have mastered the means of staying in power forever. The Islamic

Republic's tenure has been a turbulent one. In its first decade, the theocracy had to battle the marginalized remnants of the revolutionary coalition that were agitating for their share of power. Then in the 1990s came the reform movement, with its enterprising efforts to conform religious ideals to pluralistic norms. Supreme Leader Ayatollah Ali Khamenei and his militant followers understood that such a reform effort would not create an Islamic democracy but would lead to the extinction of the Islamic Republic. And then came the titanic Green Movement in the aftermath of the fraudulent presidential election of 2009 that shook the foundations of the state. The regime has never completely recovered from the convulsions of that summer. In 2018, Iran was once more rocked by demonstrations that began with economic grievances but quickly led to calls for the overthrow of the theocracy. Still, Khomeini's unusual amalgamation of clerical ruling bodies coexisting with less consequential elected institutions was an ingenious manner of protecting his revolution. It is an enterprise that will one day come to an end. But its sheer longevity is a tribute to his innovative approach to founding a political regime.

Yet another facet of the Islamic Republic is its uncanny ability to renew its constituency in the Iranian polity. A revolution usually fades when those who were present at the creation pass from the scene and a new generation of leaders inevitably looks to different sources of authority and legitimacy to underpin its rule. In the 1990s, Iran gave the impression that it would be following the model of China and other revolutionary states that eventually transcend their founding dogmas. Intellectuals, businessmen, and technocrats dominated the public sphere as

Iran seemed to be distancing itself from its revolutionary heritage. The clerical reformers were speaking of an Islamic democracy while the younger generation was moving away from a political culture that celebrated martyrdom and spiritual devotion. Beneath the surface of reform and change, however, was another segment of society: pious young men, many of them veterans of the extreme violence of the Iran-Iraq War, who remained committed to Khomeini's original vision. From this segment of society emerged men such as Ahmadinejad and diplomat Saeed Jalili, to provide a second wave of true believers in Khomeini's original ideology.

A strong strain of nostalgia motivates this younger generation of conservatives. In their publications and declarations, they tend to romanticize the 1980s as the pristine decade of ideological purity and national solidarity. Its adherents saw it as an era when the entire nation was united behind the cause of the Islamic Republic. Khomeini and his disciples were dedicated public servants free of corruption and crass competition for power, traits that would hardly characterize many of their successors. Self-reliance and self-sufficiency were cherished values of a nation that sought to mold a new Middle East. As with all idealized recollections, the conservatives' view of the 1980s has a limited connection to reality. But it is an invented past—a manufactured reality—that continues to draw a segment of the public to the theocratic state.

It is impossible to determine what portion of the Iranian public supports the revolution and its mission of ensuring God's will on earth. Given all that we know about the cultural tastes, political aspirations, and cosmopolitan nature of Iranian society, it is likely to be a small minority. Still, it is a minority tied together by religious networks, state patronage, and a sense of being under siege by the forces of change. The toxic mixture of radical religion and strident nationalism continues to attract some portion of the younger generation to Khomeini's cause. These people find material benefits in his state and a sense of salvation in his ideology. Marxism promised its adherents rewards here on earth, while Islamism calls for sacrifices that will be redeemed in the afterlife. After decades of failed experimentation, it was easy to prove that Marxism had not succeeded and that it could not transcend the forces of history. It is harder to demonstrate conclusively that Islamism cannot deliver on its celestial promises.

All this discussion of ideology and institutional juggernauts should not obscure the centrality of terror in sustaining the Islamic Republic. The regime's main enforcers are the Revolutionary Guards, the 125,000-strong shock troops commanded by the ideologues who stand committed to the values and philosophical outlook of the militant clerics. Throughout the 1990s, they called for the suppression of the reform movement and denounced its attempts to expand the political rights of the citizenry. The Guards were unleashed to deal with student protests in the summer of 1999 and pressed the leadership to violently dispense with the pro-democratic forces. And they were critical to the repression of the Green Movement in 2009. As they gained stature and wealth, the Guards emerged in the 1990s as an independent pillar of the state whose predilections and demands cannot be ignored by the ruling authorities.

Beyond the Guards, the regime has created an overlapping set of intelligence services to ensure internal security. Iran in many ways resembles East Germany, whose intelligence organization, the Stasi, spied on every aspect of its citizens' lives. Children are encouraged to denounce their parents, teachers their students, and friends their companions. Iran's intelligence organs are adept at using technology as well as old-fashioned surveillance methods to monitor any hint of opposition. They have also been behind some of the regime's most fantastic claims, such as that Western powers are using culture and commerce to foster regime-change in Iran. The paranoid culture of the Islamic Republic is most obvious among its enforcers. It is an article of faith in the hard-line circles that all American presidents, including Barack Obama, are inveterate regime-changers whose hostility to the theocracy is relentless and immutable.

The Islamic Republic has fared better than the shah in constructing a terror apparatus. The shah had created a system of government that could not function without his direct participation. All decisions had to be made by the shah. Once he collapsed, mentally and physically, at the height of the revolution, his formidable army dwindled with him. The Iranian generals were essentially second-tier men who proved as indecisive as the monarch whom they served. The Iranian revolutionaries were knocking on a hollowed-out façade. Once the shah demonstrated that he was a confused and defeated man incapable of making difficult decisions, his reign came to a quick and largely bloodless end.

Given the ideological nature of the Islamic Republic, its officer corps and intelligence functionaries have usually acted with strength and have seemed capable of taking independent action. In the summer of 2009, however, some of the hidden vulnerabilities of the regime came to the surface. Khamenei initially seemed hesitant and unsure of himself. The early moves to repress the protests originated as much in the security services as in the halls of government. Still, there was a purge of some Revolutionary Guard commanders, indicating that the task of shooting at one's own countrymen had taxed the mettle of at least some of the state enforcers. The regime did eventually come together to present a unified front against the demonstrators. Unlike the shah's army, the mullahs found enough men with little compunction about committing mass murder. Since its inception, the Islamic Republic has been adept at recruiting young men, imbued with religious fervor and buttressed by state patronage, into its Guard corps. Still, how the regime would be able to deal with a long-term, nationwide protest movement remains an open question.

The Islamic Republic has endured and sustained its revolution long past the time that many of its critics anticipated. Khomeini proved a more capable revolutionary than his more illustrious counterparts, who commanded larger and more powerful nations such as Russia and China. He misused religion and created overweening clerical bodies and an impressive terror machine to ensure the durability of his revolution. As significant as these domestic developments have been, one should not ignore the role that foreign policy has played in reinforcing the revolution at home. It is to that subject that we now turn our attention.

How Foreign Policy Has Sustained the Revolution at Home

NEARLY FORTY YEARS AFTER AYATOLLAH RUHOLLAH KHOMEINI came to power, and two decades after his death, the Islamic Republic remains an outlier in international relations. Other non-Western, revolutionary regimes eventually eschewed a rigidly ideological foreign policy and accepted the fundamental legitimacy of the international system. But Iran's leaders have remained committed to Khomeini's worldview. The resilience of Iran's Islamist ideology in the country's foreign policy is striking. Iran's leadership clings to policies derived largely from Khomeini's ideological vision, even when such policies are detrimental to the country's other stated national interests.

Many Western observers of Iran don't appreciate how Iran's foreign policy has been fashioned largely to sustain an ideological identity at home. We cannot understand Iran's foreign relations and its evident hostility to the West merely by assessing its international environment or the changing power balance in the Middle East. These things matter, but Iran's revolutionary elite also seeks to buttress the regime's ideological identity by embracing a confrontational posture. To understand this, it helps to review recent Iranian history, beginning with Khomeini's thoughts and actions.

Khomeini offered a unique challenge to the concept of the nation-state and the prevailing norms of the international system. The essence of his message was that the vitality of his Islamist vision at home was contingent on its relentless export. Moreover, because God's vision was not to be confined to a single nation, Iran's foreign policy would be an extension of its domestic revolutionary turmoil. For the grand ayatollah, the global order was divided between two competing entities: states whose priorities were defined by Western conventions and Iran, whose ostensible purpose was to redeem a divine mandate.

Khomeini's internationalism required Iran to have an antagonist, a foil against which it could define itself. A caricatured concept of the West became the central pillar of his Islamist internationalism. The Western powers were rapacious imperialists determined to exploit Iran's wealth for their own aggrandizement. Islamist themes soon followed, portraying the West as also seeking to subjugate Muslims and impose its cultural template on other countries in the name of modernity. Disunity among Muslims, the autocracies populating the region, the failure of the clerical class to assume the mantle of opposition, and young people's attraction to alien ideologies were seen as by-products of a Western plot to sustain dominance over Islam's realm. Four episodes from the 1980s underscore how foreign policy was used to buttress the ideological transformation at home: the 1979–81 hostage crisis; the war with Iraq; the events surrounding the Salman Rushdie fatwa; and a Khomeini-ordered massacre of political prisoners.

It is often forgotten that those in charge during the initial stages of the 1979 revolution were not Khomeini's clerical militants. Amid an ongoing power struggle between the clerics and the provisional government's moderates, the Iranian government did not seek to break ties with the United States. Although Tehran would not be a pawn in the US-Soviet conflict, it wished to maintain normal diplomatic and economic relations with Washington.

Thus, Khomeini and his clerical allies increasingly saw the provisional government as an impediment to their larger objectives. The task of redrafting the constitution along radical lines and electing a cleric-dominated parliament required displacing the provisional government. At the end of the day, this combination of concerns pressed the radicals around Khomeini to provoke a crisis that would galvanize the populace behind the cause of the Islamic Republic and its ideological precepts.

On November 4, 1979, a group of Iranian students breached the walls of the US embassy and captured sixty-six Americans. They remained hostage for 444 days. The embassy takeover provided Khomeini with the opportunity to inflame popular sentiment and claim that external enemies, aided and abetted by domestic accomplices, were plotting against the revolution. To a frenzied populace, it seemed plausible that the United States was up to mischief. The students enabled this narrative by painstakingly piecing together shredded embassy documents and selectively releasing them to the press. The Iranian public rushed to the defense of the revolution and Prime Minister

Mehdi Bazargan and the members of his provisional government tendered their resignations.

On December 2, 1979, a draft constitution favored by Khomeini, which granted essential power to the unelected branches of government, was submitted to the public. Khomeini warned that its rejection at such a critical juncture would demonstrate signs of disunity and provoke an attack by the United States. The regime's propaganda machine insisted that only secular intellectuals tied to US imperialism were averse to the governing document. It worked: fully 99 percent of the population voted for the constitution.

Out of this crisis emerged two other factors, namely the clerics' quest to usher in a militant foreign policy and their desire to strike a psychological blow against the United States. The provisional government's approach to international relations had been strict nonalignment with a willingness to pursue normal relations with the United States. This formulation was explicitly rejected by the newly empowered militants who provoked the hostage crisis in order to foster a different international orientation. The Bazargan government's resignation ended that brief interlude of moderation. Under a more radical orientation, Iran's foreign policy would become not merely an abstention from taking sides in the superpower conflict but an assertion of radical Islamism as the foundation of the nation's foreign policy. Through a symbolic attack on the US embassy, the new revolutionaries not only consolidated their domestic power but also demonstrated their contempt for prevailing international norms. Iran now would inveigh against the United States, assist belligerent actors throughout the Middle

East, and plot against the state of Israel. Terrorism became a tool for the liberation of the so-called oppressed.

Iran's war with Iraq was the next big event in this saga of the Iranian elite's resolve to meld domestic and foreign policy. The triumph of Iran's revolution, with its denial of the legitimacy of the prevailing order and its calls for the reformulation of the state structure along religious lines, portended conflict with neighboring states. Revolutions are frequently followed by war, as newly empowered elites look abroad for the redemption of their cause. In Iran, the new elite mixed aggressive propaganda, subversion, and terrorism to advance its cause in Iraq, where minority Sunnis dominated a majority Shiite population. Perhaps nowhere was Iran's message of Shiite empowerment received with greater acclaim than among Iraqi Shiites. Tehran denounced the legitimacy of the Baathist government, openly called for a Shiite revolution similar to its own that toppled the shah, and seemed to have contact with various Shiite opposition forces. Hovering over all this was the existing border dispute, in which Iraq was compelled by the shah in 1975 to concede to Iran's demands on territorial divisions. Saddam Hussein always despised that agreement and saw it as an act of humiliation that he had to accept, given the disparity of power at that time between Iran and Iraq. Iran's provocative behavior and Saddam's sense of grievance and opportunism finally pushed him to invade Iran in 1980, which ignited one of the region's most devastating conflicts.

The Iranian clerical state didn't measure progress in the Iran-Iraq War in traditional categories like territory lost or gained, boundary demarcations, or reparation offers. Rather, it saw the war as an opportunity to merge its religious pedigree with its nationalist claims. The war was viewed in Iran as an assault on Islam and the Prophet's legacy by profane forces of disbelief. The clerical estate genuinely identified itself with the Prophet's mission and saw Saddam's secular regime as yet another manifestation of inauthenticity and corruption. Iran had not been attacked because of its provocations or lingering territorial disputes, but because it embodied Islam and sought to carry out the Prophet's injunctions. Thus, it was the moral obligation of the citizenry to defend Iran as if it were safeguarding Islam itself.

By June 1982, Iran had reversed Iraq's early gains and had essentially evicted the invaders from its territory. The Iranian leaders then had to confront whether or not to continue the war by carrying the fight into Iraq. Given the war's economic costs and human toll, the decision to attack Iraq remains one of the most contentious in Iran's modern history. In its many commemorations of the war, the state has acknowledged in its various official histories that more than five million Iranians served in the war, with 220,000 dead. Khomeini resolutely dismissed various offers for a cease-fire and generous reparations. Instead, Iran embraced a disastrous extension of the conflict based on a combination of ideological conviction, the misperception that the war could be terminated quickly, and a fear that Saddam would not remain contained for long.

The rationales underlying Iran's decision to prolong the war are still debated widely. The conventional view discounts the notion that prolonging the war was seen as a means of consolidating the revolution at home. But Khomeini soon celebrated the decision as a "third revolution" whose purpose was not just to repel the invaders but also to cleanse Iran of all secular tendencies. In order to exploit the war politically, the state had to present the conflict in distinctly religious terms. A revolutionary order seeking to usher in a new era could not wage a limited war designed to achieve carefully calibrated objectives. The war had to be a crusade. In fact, it needed to be a rebellion against the forces of iniquity and impiety. Through collective sacrifice and spiritual redemption, the theocratic regime would fend off the invaders, change the character of Iran once and for all, and project power throughout the region.

The war ultimately ended for the same reason it was prolonged: the need to sustain the revolution at home. By 1988, Iran was exhausted and weary from having waged an eight-year war without any measurable international support. Iraqi counterattacks and the war of cities—in which Iraq threatened Iranian urban centers with ballistic missile bombardment and potentially chemical weapons—undermined the arguments for war. The stringencies of war were compounded by a decline in the pool of volunteers that undercut Iran's strategy of utilizing manpower to overcome Iraq's technological superiority. The inability of Iran to muster sufficient volunteers meant it had to embark on a more rigorous conscription effort that further estranged the population. Continuation of the war threatened the revolution and perhaps even the regime.

The war left a significant imprint on Iran's international orientation. The quest for self-sufficiency and self-reliance is a hallmark of the Islamic Republic's foreign policy, as the guardians of the revolution recognized that their regime's survival depended entirely on their own efforts. International organizations, global opinion, and prevailing conventions did not protect Iran from Iraq's chemical-weapons assaults. Saddam's aggression, targeting of civilians, persistent interference with Persian Gulf commerce, and use of weapons of mass destruction were all condoned—and perhaps even abetted—by the great powers. Thus, the war went a long way toward imposing the clerical template on Iran's ruling system.

As Khomeini approached the end of his life, he grew apprehensive about the vitality of his revolution. Suddenly there was a risk that the vanguard Islamic Republic would become a tempered and moderate state. Iran would, in short, experience the same cycle of revolution and reaction that other revolutionary regimes from the eighteenth through the twentieth centuries had experienced. China was a cautionary model as, soon after the death of Mao, it moved in a pragmatic direction of discarding his ideological legacy. At this point, Khomeini undertook two specific acts to ensure that his disciples would sustain his revolutionary radicalism and resist moderation. In 1988, shortly after the cease-fire with Iraq, he ordered one of his last acts of bloodletting: the execution of thousands of political prisoners then languishing in Iran's jails. The mass executions, carried out over several months, were designed to test Khomeini's supporters and make certain that they were ruthlessly committed to his revolution. Those who showed hesitancy would be seen as halfhearted and dismissed from power. And this indeed did happen to Ayatollah Hossein Ali Montazeri, who objected. Khomeini was confident that the government he would leave behind had the courage to inflict massive and arbitrary terror to maintain power. Even after this bloodletting, however, he still worried about possible backsliding on relations with the West.

Khomeini, therefore, manufactured another external crisis to stoke the revolutionary fires. The publication of Salman Rushdie's *Satanic Verses*, which depicted the Prophet Muhammad in an unflattering light, offered a perfect opportunity. In February 1989, Khomeini issued his infamous fatwa offering a bounty for the deaths of Rushdie and his publishers. Numerous bombings and acts of violence followed the issuance of the edict, including the death of twelve people in a large anti-Rushdie riot in India. However, the fatwa was cynically designed to radicalize the Iranian masses in support of the regime's ideology. While the international community saw his act as an indication of his intolerance and militancy, Khomeini considered domestic political calculations to be paramount. Iran was once more globally ostracized, a development entirely acceptable—even desirable—to Khomeini.

On June 3, 1989, one of the most militant and successful revolutionaries in history died. Khomeini breathed his last, confident that his republic and his ideology would survive. Although many external observers appeared certain that the inevitable process of moderation would set in to tame the revolutionary fervor of the Iranian regime, it was not to be. The Islamic Republic's commitment to the revolution has remained remarkably resilient.

THE RAFSANJANI YEARS: PRAGMATISM
AND ITS DISCONTENTS

With the end of the prolonged war with Iraq and Khomeini's death, Iran's focus shifted from external peril to its own domestic quandaries. The 1990s became one of the most important periods of stalled transition to pragmatism for the Islamic Republic. It was also a period of intense factionalism. The new president, Ali Akbar Hashemi Rafsanjani, and his allies sensed that for the Islamic Republic to survive, it had to craft a new national compact and reestablish its legitimacy. Iran had to restructure its economy and provide for the practical needs of its people. It also had to adjust to the international realities that were the result of the collapse of the Soviet Union and the 1991 Gulf War. To realize his vision of economic renovation, Rafsanjani sought to mend fences with the neighboring Gulf states and reach out to the European Union and Russia. But the United States remained out of bounds. The so-called Great Satan was still the rallying cry of a revolution born out of a high-octane animosity toward America.

Standing against Rafsanjani and his cohort was a conservative faction led by Khomeini's successor, Supreme Leader Ali Khamenei. This faction appreciated that a relaxation of tensions was necessary in the aftermath of the war, due to economic demands. But its international outlook continued to be influenced by the need to sustain Iran's Islamist ideology. This became all the more pressing as many Iranians began to move beyond the revolutionary legacy and seek a new future. Given this popular challenge, the conservatives became even more invested in rejecting normalization with the West for fear that such a move would provoke cultural subversion that would further erode the foundations of the state. The dual themes of Great Satan and the "clash of civilizations" underscored their pronouncements and defined their political identity. The West remained a sinister source of cultural pollution whose temptations had to be resisted even more strenuously after Khomeini's death and the emergence in Iran of popular interest in Western ways and vogues. The fact that Iran's youth no longer paid attention to ponderous theological musings was immaterial to a political class that perceived its legitimacy as deriving from God's will. Foreign policy was, paradoxically, seen as a way of isolating Iran from the international integration that this class feared. Iran would now move in opposing directions, confounding both its critics and its supporters.

The self-defeating nature of Iran's foreign policy was evident in the Persian Gulf. Iran behaved moderately during the American campaign to evict Iraq from Kuwait. Some of the members of the clerical leadership took the rash step of calling for Iran to side with its old nemesis Iraq against the greater American threat. Rafsanjani and Khamenei disregarded such reckless pronouncements. In the aftermath of the war, Iran began discussing a regional security arrangement, whereby the stability of the Gulf would be undertaken by the local actors. This was a clever way of ensuring Iranian hegemony and seeking the expulsion of the US Navy from the Gulf. Such measures were obviously unacceptable to the Saudis and other Gulf sheikhdoms that had no intention of subordinating themselves to Iran.

Once Iran's regional schemes were rebuffed, it reverted to form. From the Islamic Republic's platforms, the clerical oligarchs continued to inveigh against the Gulf's princely class and called upon the Shiites of the Gulf to revolt. Iran continued to pursue subversive activities and terrorism, including the 1996 bombing of the Khobar Towers' US Air Force housing unit in Saudi Arabia. Nineteen US servicemen were killed in the attack. While the Islamic Republic publicly emphasized diplomacy and cooperation, it also engaged in incendiary propaganda and acts of terror.

A similar pattern was seen when Rafsanjani attempted to improve relations with Europe. Iran's need for foreign technologies and investments propelled the new outlook. The European states initially embraced the new Iranian president and responded to his overtures with a policy of "critical dialogue," which suggested that Iran could be persuaded to modify its behavior through diplomatic discussions and economic incentives. But the death sentence on Rushdie and the assassination of Iranian dissidents on European soil militated against better relations.

Rafsanjani did try to tone down the Rushdie affair by suggesting that although Khomeini's decree could not be countermanded, Iran would not necessarily carry out the order. Iranian politicians, who insisted that the fatwa was irreversible, soon contradicted these statements. Iran's powerful religious foundations maintained bounties on Rushdie's head and Britain actually expelled a number of Iranian diplomats on the suspicion that they were plotting Rushdie's murder. Iran's inability to separate itself from Khomeini's decree obstructed its attempt to mend fences with Europe.

Terror still remained an instrument of Iran's policy in Europe, as reflected in the assassination of Kurdish dissidents in the Berlin restaurant Mykonos. The German judiciary blamed Iran for the attack, particularly its Ministry of Intelligence and Security. As a result, the European states all withdrew their envoys from Iran. Ultimately, Iran's failure to craft a different relationship with accommodating Europeans reflected its inability to emancipate itself from its revolutionary legacy.

It is customary to attribute the contradictions in Iran's foreign policy to domestic factionalism. The pragmatists were seen as attempting to move the state in one direction, only to be beset by hard-liners. The internal factionalism was all too real and Rafsanjani's outlook certainly differed from that of Khamenei. And, to be sure, there is much that we don't know about Iran's opaque decision-making process. But Rafsanjani was known as a politician who seldom had the courage of his own convictions. As president, he must have been involved in the Islamic Republic's terrorist activities. Even if he thought them unwise, he did nothing to stop them.

For the hard-liners who despised the Gulf rulers as America's lackeys and distrusted Europeans as agents of cultural subversion, terrorism was an effective way of lashing out. They relished isolation, for it was only in such a stark environment that the revolution could be nurtured at home. Moreover, as with most ideologues, they believed that acts of violence might trigger an uprising among the Gulf Shiites that would displace the incumbent monarchies. The violence against Iranian dissidents in Europe can only be seen through the prism of Iran's paranoid politics. Although external opposition forces did not have much constituency in Iran, the regime still waged terror campaigns against them in Europe. Isolation from the international community was a penalty they were willing to pay.

The one policy area where Rafsanjani's pragmatism prevailed was relations with the Russian Federation. Like many Third World countries struggling for autonomy within the international order, Iran found the collapse of the Soviet Union initially disturbing. That turned to alarm among the clerical elite with the massive deployment of US forces to the Persian Gulf and the expressed American commitment to contain "outlaw" or "pariah state" regimes. As a price for strategic support and access to Russian arms, the Islamic Republic made its own adjustments to the emergence of an independent Central Asia. In a rare display of judiciousness, Iran largely tempered its ideology, stressing the importance of trade and stability rather than the propagation of its Islamist message. The full scope of Iranian pragmatism became evident during the Chechnya conflict. At a time when Russian soldiers were massacring Muslim rebels and civilians indiscriminately, Iran merely declared the issue to be an internal Russian matter.

Several factors propelled Iran toward such realism. First, many within the clerical elite perceived that Central Asia was not really susceptible to Iran's Islamist message. Iran's aversion to isolation also played a part. The fact that Iran could not craft better relations with the United States, and was largely isolated from both Europe and the Gulf sheikhdoms, made ties with

Moscow an imperative. For the conservatives, one way of fending off American pressure and European displeasure was cultivating close economic and security ties with Russia. Thus, the Russian Federation became the beneficiary of Iran's failure to develop a more coherent policy toward other global actors.

During Rafsanjani's tenure, Iran moved gingerly beyond the rigid parameters of the 1980s. Pragmatism and calibration of national interests became considerations in Iran's foreign policy decision-making. Yet ideology never was eclipsed by pragmatic calculations. For many members of the Islamic Republic's elite, their charge remained the realization of Khomeini's Islamist vision at home. They therefore desired Iran's estrangement from the West while avoiding any crisis that would threaten the regime. It was a difficult balancing act in which terrorism served a useful purpose by provoking Western sanctions and opprobrium but not much more. Thus, the clerical oligarchs manufactured an atmosphere of external threat to sustain their power and preserve the essential identity of their state.

On January 8, 2017, Rafsanjani died, eliciting much Western adoration. The US State Department even issued its own condolences—a first for a leader who ordered the death of many Americans, including the servicemen in the Khobar Towers. The obituaries credited Rafsanjani with attempts to reach out to America and establish a more tolerant regime at home. Such misperceptions failed to note that Iran did not fundamentally change during Rafsanjani's tenure. The lesson: should an Iranian leader merely temper his rhetoric, he could count on much forbearance from the liberal salons in the United States and the West.

TEHRAN SPRING

The most momentous attempt to change Iran's foreign policy came with the 1997 election of the reformist president Mohammad Khatami. The aim of Khatami and the reform movement was not merely to make the theocracy more accountable to its citizenry, but also to end the Islamic Republic's pariah status and integrate it into global society. Given his overwhelming popular mandate and seeming determination, Khatami presented a unique challenge to Khamenei and the conservatives. While the reformist forces wanted reconciliation with Saudi Arabia, normalized relations with the European Union, and outreach to the United States, Khamenei accepted only the first two of these measures. He understood that Iran's national interests required a different relationship with its neighbors and its European commercial partners. Moreover, the conservatives, initially shell-shocked by Khatami's unexpected triumph, yielded only warily to his early measures.

Khatami's "good neighbor" diplomacy rehabilitated Iran's ties with the Gulf regimes. Numerous trade, diplomatic, and security agreements were signed between the Islamic Republic and the Gulf sheikhdoms. Iran ceased its support for opposition forces operating in those countries. Abdullah bin Abdulaziz al Saud, then crown prince of Saudi Arabia, seemed receptive to such overtures and the two parties began a dialogue on critical issues. Khatami managed, at least momentarily, to transcend Khomeini's divisive legacy and replace ideological antagonisms with policies rooted in realistic self-interest. From the outset, however, the new rapprochement appeared tentative, as the Gulf sheikhdoms remained suspicious and the hard-liners in Iran nurtured their antagonisms.

Khatami's cautious domestic liberalization similarly expedited détente with the European states. He ended the long-standing practice of assassinating Iranian dissidents in Europe. Also, the issue of the Rushdie fatwa was finally settled, as Khatami pledged that Iran would not enforce the edict. After years of living underground, the beleaguered author was able to pursue a more normal life and resume his literary pursuits. European envoys returned to Iran and Iran's president was welcomed in European capitals.

Khatami's approach to America was more carefully crafted and was gingerly executed. Conscious of the conservatives' deep-seated reservations, he sought to ease mutual suspicion through a gradual exchange of scholars, activists, and athletes. He hoped US economic concessions might provide him with sufficient leverage to influence the conservatives at home, particularly the wary supreme leader. The Clinton administration was prepared for an unconditional dialogue with Iran, and private messages were exchanged. But Khatami underestimated the extent of the hard-liners' hostility to any thaw in US-Iranian relations. From the conservatives' perspective, Khatami and the reformers' enterprising moves were beginning to endanger a revolution that relied on isolation to thrive.

Soon, a conservative counterstrategy began to crystallize. The conservatives employed their control over various governmental and parastatal institutions to negate parliamentary legislation designed to liberalize Iran's polity. The judiciary imprisoned prominent reformers and closed down their newspapers.

Vigilante and terror groups harassed student gatherings and assassinated prominent intellectuals. And foreign policy once again came into play. Conservatives dismissed the reform movement's ability to deliver on its promises as a means of undermining international confidence in Khatami's government. Terrorism reemerged as a means of advancing the conservative agenda and subverting reformist plans.

The 9/11 tragedies and subsequent American interventions in the Middle East provoked competing impulses in Tehran. The speed of the American invasion of Afghanistan shocked the leaders of the Islamic Republic. They had assumed that the United States would become entangled in Afghanistan for some time to come. The "graveyard of empires" did not consume the latest occidental invaders. Still, the displacement of the Taliban, a radical Sunni group that nearly went to war with Iran in 1998, offered the theocracy a friendlier Afghanistan. A combination of fear and opportunism caused Iran to behave responsibly and it participated in various international conferences to aid the fledgling Afghan government.

The next chapter in the post-9/11 saga—the American invasion of Iraq—further unsettled the Islamist regime. These were heady days in the Middle East, with America's shock-and-awe campaign intimidating recalcitrant actors into accommodation. "No one thought that Saddam's regime would fall in three weeks. The military leadership had anticipated that Saddam would not fall easily and that America would have to fight the Iraqi army for at least six months to a year before reaching Saddam," recalled then secretary to the Supreme National Security Council Hassan Rouhani.[2] Yet the proximity of

American guns compelled the theocracy to act with caution. Iran now commenced negotiations with the European states and suspended the clandestine nuclear program that was first revealed by an opposition group in August 2002. Tehran also made gestures of being cooperative in Iraq, just as it had been in Afghanistan.

The pragmatism that Iran exhibited between 2001 and 2003 could be described as moderation under compulsion. As the Bush administration unfurled a doctrine that called the nexus of terrorism and weapons of mass destruction the greatest threat to the United States, the Iranian regime took notice. Iran was the world's leading sponsor of terrorism and was secretly developing an elaborate nuclear infrastructure. The regime felt imperiled and saw wisdom in circumspection. It presented Khatami as its spokesperson and suspended key aspects of its nuclear program. Its cagey diplomats attended international conferences hinting at support to come. But Iran did not change its ideological stripes—it merely hunkered down until the storm passed.

Iran's conduct during this period has had an important impact on the perennial international relations debate about how to moderate ideological regimes. The proponents of détente argued that providing incentives and offers of dialogue could create a basis for moderation. The more hawkish skeptics claimed that such regimes are devoted to the fundamentals of their ideology and that pressure is the only means to ensure their compliance with international norms. Iran's case demonstrates that revolutionary regimes are not likely to be tempted into moderation by incentives. Europe's policy of "critical dialogue" was premised on the notion that rewards would temper Iran and empower its moderate forces. Yet, Iran's response was one of defiance, as it launched a nuclear program in secret and conducted assassination campaigns on European soil. The Bush administration's credible threats had far more impact, as it got Iran to suspend its nuclear program and behave with a measure of responsibility in the region. America's adversaries regained their confidence once the Bush doctrine disappeared in the sandstorms of Iraq and America found itself in a quagmire that sapped its strength.

IRAN'S NEW FRONTIERS

The 2005 presidential election put an end to the reformist interlude and the attempt to make the Iranian theocracy more tolerant at home and reasonable abroad. A new generation of conservative political figures assumed the mantle of revolutionary leadership. This was a war generation, veterans who had served on the front lines and were dismayed by the Islamic Republic's move away from its revolutionary idealism. As uncompromising nationalists, they were sensitive to Iran's prerogatives and sovereign rights. As committed Islamists, they saw the Middle East as a battleground between forces of secularism and Islamic authenticity. As emerging national leaders, they perceived Western conspiracies where none existed.

"We must return to the roots of the revolution," proclaimed presidential candidate Mahmoud Ahmadinejad during his campaign.[3] It seemed like yet another empty promise by yet another politician brandishing retrogressive shibboleths in the hope of mobilizing his constituents. A theocratic state riddled with corruption had generated a degree of popular cynicism. Even genuine expressions of revolutionary convictions were treated with skepticism. Ahmadinejad in many ways seemed an anachronism, as he believed that the government of God still had relevance. And he was earnest in his perception that all of the country's problems could be solved if only Iran went back to the roots of the revolution.

Ahmadinejad's presidency was a rebuke to reformers who had grown cautious and complacent. For Iran to be revitalized and reawakened, its leaders had to capture the moral cohesion and stern discipline of those who bravely confronted Saddam's war machine. The instrument of Iran's redemption had to be Islam—not the passive, indifferent Islam of the reformist establishment but the revolutionary, politicized, and uncompromising devotion that launched the initial Islamic Republic. A united Iranian populace would once more redeem its faith from the transgressions of the West. By appropriating Islam's sacred symbols and invoking the history of struggle against foreign infidels and their domestic enablers, Ahmadinejad sought to transform religion once more into a revolutionary ideology. Such a faith would galvanize the masses to reclaim their lost republic and defend their patrimony.

The younger militants found patrons in the clerical hardliners led by Khamenei. Iran's conservatives, old and young, are imbued with an anti-American spirit. The United States is seen as an imperial aggressor trampling on the Middle East and a source of cultural pollution. Democracy is a subversive tool for undermining the Islamic Republic. Integration into the global economy is a sinister means of making Iran dependent on foreigners. In a sense, the hard-liners have offered their constituents their own social contract, whereby in exchange for spiritual devotion, the public will relinquish the right to dissent.

Iran's revolutionary resurgence coincided with America's difficulties in pacifying Iraq and Afghanistan. As the United States became bogged down in Iraq and divided at home, Iran began to press its claims in the region. Iran now subsidized a range of Shiite actors, organized militias that were responsive to Tehran's dictates, and instigated violence against US troops. In the meantime, it ended the suspension of its nuclear program and abjured American offers of talks. The consolidation of the revolution needed victories, and Iran's inroads into Iraq and the resumption of its nuclear enrichment activities provided a narrative of success.

In light of all this, the 2009 presidential election posed a stark choice for Iran. It could opt for a return to reformist policies and an effort to become part of the community of nations by accepting the norms of the international community, or it could embark on the "New Right" path of self-assertion and defiance. The public clearly preferred the former path, but the governing elite chose the latter. The fraudulent reelection of Ahmadinejad provoked not just protests and demonstrations, but forever delegitimized the Islamic Republic. The gap between state and society was wide and remains unbridged. A broad mass of the Iranian public does not share the ideological fervor of the ruling elite.

Ahmadinejad's second term was beset by economic decline stemming from the stalemated negotiations over Iran's nuclear program. Iran's defiance at the negotiating table was causing it serious financial difficulties that could potentially endanger the regime. The international sanctions effort orchestrated by the United States had cut off Iran from access to international financial markets and its usual customers. The Europeans had ceased to purchase its oil, insure its tankers, and facilitate its financial transactions. By 2012, Iran's economy had shrunk by 20 percent and its currency was in free fall. The revolution seemed in real danger of extinction.

The 2013 presidential election was bound to focus on the issue of nuclear diplomacy at a time of such persistent economic decline. Rouhani, a longtime stalwart of the regime who had once led the nuclear negotiations himself, stepped forward with a message of pragmatism. Iran had to solve the nuclear issue on acceptable terms as a means of revitalizing its economy. A nuclear accord was seen as reinforcing the revolution at home. But that was not all, as an arms control agreement was also seen as critical to the Islamic Republic's imperial project.

In the twenty-first century, the Middle East has offered Iran ample opportunities to project its power. The postcolonial Arab state system has all but collapsed and state failures in Syria and Iraq offered Iran an opening to strengthen its sectarian allies. Such projections of power may have been tempting, but they were also costly. Ironically, for Iran to become a great power, it had to dispense with the nuclear issue that was financially draining the state. Still, the Islamic Republic was not about to shut down its nuclear program as it sought an accord that recognized its right to enrich uranium while stipulating that it could industrialize its enrichment program after a period of time.

The Joint Comprehensive Plan of Action (JCPOA) granted Iran all that it needed. Rouhani had succeeded in preserving the program, ensuring its future expansion, and getting rid of the sanctions regime crafted over a decade. This was a triumph for his brand of revolutionary diplomacy.

The election of Rouhani was neither a rebuke to Khamenei nor an indication that the revolution had finally exhausted itself. The regime had consolidated its power and reached a consensus on important issues. The reformist interlude was all but over, and Rouhani would not shake the foundations of the state by insisting on its liberalization. The onerous cultural restrictions that so agitated the youth of Iran would remain intact. Human rights would be abused and dissent punished. The Islamic Republic would continue to preserve its regional equities and would engage in negotiations with the United States only if those talks served its purpose. The regime had finally reached an internal agreement on foreign policy issues. Iran would continue its regional expansion while sustaining its hostility to the United States and Israel. The revolution had come full circle and dispensed with some of the issues that so often divided the state against itself.

The one aspect of Rouhani's tenure that damaged the revolution was rampant corruption and class differences that were becoming even wider. The nuclear agreement did fill Iran's financial coffers, but much of that money was being sniffed off to foreign adventures and elite corruption. In a government that is ostensibly devoted to the cause of religion, such ostentatious corruption is bound to further diminish the regime's tattered legitimacy.

As Ali Khamenei celebrates his more than quarter-century as the supreme leader, he stands as one of the most successful imperialists in Iran's modern history. The shah, even at the height of his power, did not have a commanding position in Iraq and the Persian Gulf. The politics of Lebanon largely eluded him and Syria remained outside his reach. As the region has changed since the Arab Spring, Iran's international orientation has also altered in subtle ways. For decades, the theocratic rulers presented themselves as agents of pan-Islamism and rejected the charge of sectarianism. Although Iran continues to denounce religious division from its official podiums, its actual policy is to empower Shiite actors who share its disdain for incumbent Sunni Arab regimes. Shiite imperialism, not lofty pan-Islamism, is now conditioning Iran's regional policy.

The Islamic Republic's refurbished Shiite chauvinism holds great promise to its remaining constituents. For centuries, Persian monarchs and mullahs have seen Iran as the epicenter of the region's politics, a natural hegemon for a disorderly Middle East. It was a role that the occidental powers arrogated to themselves, but in the end neither the British nor the American empires could discharge that obligation. They were too culturally distant, too infatuated with their Western paradigms of development, and too ignorant of the slippery politics of the Middle East. The sun has long set on the British Empire, and an America humbled in Iraq is wrestling with its own limitations of power. In its chronicle of empowerment, Iran stood toe to toe with America during the arms control negotiations and obtained a grudging admission from all the great powers that it has a right to nuclear parity. Iran is the most consequential regional power whose claims cannot be ignored. Yet it is still hard to see whether imperialism can save a revolution that has exhausted itself. The great surge of Soviet power in the 1970s did little to sustain communism. Still, in the region's tumult, the members of the theocracy see a pathway to enable the revolutionary narrative and steady the regime.

For imperialism to be successful, it has to avoid the costly traps that eventually devoured the Kremlin. It was in the Lebanon of the 1980s that Iran first developed a model of cheap imperialism, and it is that paradigm that is guiding its policy toward the multi-confessional states of Iraq and Syria. The Islamic Republic's objectives in Lebanon were simple. First, keep the central government weak as a means of preventing the emergence of a cohesive state capable of governing all of its territory. The next step was to develop a lethal paramilitary force that could discharge violence on behalf of its Iranian patron. Hezbollah remains Iran's most enterprising and successful project, a militia that has effectively done Iran's bidding both inside and outside Lebanon. The theocratic regime also sought to subjugate the clerical order in Lebanon as a means of enhancing its own shrine cities as the centers of Shiite learning and patronage.

Soon after the US invasion of Iraq in 2003, Iran began implementing its "Lebanon model" next door in Iraq. It started by infiltrating its forces and organizing Shiite militias that operated outside the control of the governing authorities in Baghdad. Through intimidation and bribery, Iran recruited many politicians and clerics and ensured a constitutional arrangement whereby power resided in the provinces and away from the central government. In the meantime, Iran infiltrated key ministries and security services. The increased trade between the two states and millions of pilgrims crossing the border further tied Iran and Iraq together. Grand Ayatollah Ali Sistani stands as the final barrier to Iran's domination of Iraqi Shiite centers. After his death, the predicament of Iraq's seminaries will be a precarious one. All this is not to suggest that the Iraqis wish to be subordinated to Iran. But given America's reluctance to be entangled in Iraq and Baghdad's rejection by the council of Arab states, they would appear to have little choice.

Next door in Syria, the Iran-Russia-Hezbollah axis has succeeded. Once more, Iran has trained militias that the Damascus regime does not control, while Hezbollah's shock troops helped stabilize the Assad regime. Russia's airpower has been an indispensable shield as Iran and its foot soldiers made a mockery of the American proclamation that "Assad must go." It is unlikely that Bashar al-Assad will ever command the entire country, but whatever rump state he is left with will be dominated by Iran. The dream of connecting the Persian Gulf to the Mediterranean that eluded so many Persian dynasties is finally within Khamenei's grasp.

Along the way, Iran has developed an effective means of deterring the United States. It is deterrence on the cheap and relies on terrorism and arms control. During the dark days of Iraqi civil war, Shiite militias trained and armed by Iran lacerated the American troops. This has scarred the US military that now has approximately six thousand troops redeployed back in Iraq. This is just enough to be vulnerable to Iranian terror but not enough to disarm its proxies and cleanse Iraq of its nefarious influence. The Islamic Republic's strategy is obvious: should America hold Iran responsible for terrorism, it will respond with terrorism. Many influential voices in Washington are concerned that US troops in Iraq are hostage to Iranian retribution. America's appetite for negating Iran's malign strategies may yet be diminished by Tehran's terror apparatus. Terrorism was once thought of as the weapon of the weak, but in the hands of the clerical oligarchs it is rapidly becoming a doctrine of considerable deterrence.

As we have seen, since the 1979 Iranian revolution, the United States has sought to temper the Islamist regime's power by imposing economic sanctions. Successive American administrations labored hard to induce Iran's trading partners to lessen their investments and purchase of Iranian oil. America sought to segregate Iran from the global financial institutions and make its commerce more expensive. The nuclear agreement with Iran—the JCPOA—has largely disabled that tactic. Much of the text of the agreement is devoted to economic penalties that are waived, lifted, or altogether disbanded. Trade delegations and contract-signing ceremonies are now the order of the day in Tehran. It is important to stress that Iran agreed to the nuclear accord not just to gain sanctions relief, but to make it impossible for America to ever again impose a punitive sanctions regime. Too many deals are being signed and too many companies are moving into Iran for America's European partners to accede again to a sanctions regime.

All this is not to suggest that the United States is inherently at a disadvantage in confronting Iran. A bold policy of pressuring Iran must puncture these formidable obstacles and accept a measure of risk. A confrontation with Iran in the contested lands of Iraq and Syria is a possibility should Washington prove serious about limiting Tehran's pernicious influence in the region. This requires enhancement of American capabilities in terms of troops deployed in the region. A policy of imposing economic penalties on Iran for its regional aggression and domestic human rights abuses may, in fact, cause a degree of consternation among allies, which has to be managed diplomatically. The notion that America should be restrained by the JCPOA ignores the fact that the accord is a deficient agreement whose permissive technical provisions have to be revisited. Today, Iran is on a steady and legal path to the bomb.

In the end, Iran is not likely to go the way of other revolutionary states and relinquish its ideological patrimony for more mundane considerations. What is remarkable is that the Islamic Republic has managed to maintain its revolutionary identity in the face of substantial countervailing pressures, elite defections, and mass disaffection throughout the country. The institutional juggernaut of the revolution has contributed to this success, as has the elite molded in Khomeini's austere image. But Iran's foreign policy also has played a crucial role in sustaining this domestic ideological identity. The ruling elite, commanding key institutions of the state, has fashioned a foreign policy designed to maintain the ideological character of the regime. And that remains a key ingredient in determining how the Islamic Republic thinks of itself and its role in the Middle East.

3

Key Episodes in US-Iran Diplomacy

THE HISTORY OF US-IRAN RELATIONS MAY BE MARKED BY animosity, suspicion, and conflict, but it is also a history replete with its share of diplomatic engagement. Nearly every US president since the advent of the Islamic Republic in 1979 has sought negotiations with Iran. Four episodes, in particular, stand out as the most important occasions of diplomatic interchange between the two states. All four reveal that Iran has been uncanny in exploiting the talks for advancing its objectives. Throughout these talks, some US tactics worked and others did not. And nearly every administration repeated the mistakes of its predecessors and failed to learn the right lessons.

Jimmy Carter was the first American president to enter into talks with the Islamic Republic as he sought the release of US diplomats held hostage by the revolutionary regime. Carter bequeathed his successors a series of assumptions that were as wrong as they are durable. For Carter, the Islamic Republic was not a nation-state but a collection of factions competing for political power and susceptible to US influence.

That view suggests that the main task of American diplomacy was, and remains, to empower the so-called moderates. An excessively punitive policy had to be avoided for it would endanger these less extreme forces. Ronald Reagan followed suit as he sought to alter Iran's internal balance of power with arms sales in order to win the release of American citizens taken hostage in the 1980s. The George W. Bush administration came into office displaying moral contempt for the clerical autocracy, only to fall back on the old notion that the United States must find a way of engaging Iran through negotiations. No president has had more faith in diplomacy than Barack Obama, and the tragic legacy of that confidence is the worst arms control agreement in US history.

AMERICA HELD HOSTAGE

November 4, 1979, began as any other day in revolutionary Tehran, with protests engulfing the streets of the capital. But a group of demonstrating students suddenly took a different route, breaching the walls of the formidable US embassy and announcing the arrest of the perplexed diplomats. The ostensible purpose of the hostage-taking was the students' alarm that the shah's admission to the United States for medical treatment was an attempt by Washington to orchestrate a coup against Iran's nascent revolutionary regime. Carter, accustomed to Iranian transgressions, including an incident earlier that year in which the outer perimeter of the embassy had been overrun by protesters, sensed yet another momentary crisis soon to be resolved, while the officials of Iran's provisional government seemed annoyed by the students' conduct. Yet the embassy takeover very soon became entangled in Iran's labyrinthine politics, prolonging the incarceration of the diplomats for more than a year.

As we have seen, at the outset of the revolution Iran was divided against itself. The provisional government had signaled its desire to pursue a moderate foreign policy, even maintaining ties to the United States. To be sure, it did not envision an alliance with America like the one that prevailed under the shah, but the two powers could still maintain normal relations. This was the message that Prime Minister Mehdi Bazargan and his foreign minister, Ebrahim Yazdi, conveyed to Carter's national security advisor, Zbigniew Brzezinski (accompanied by his young executive assistant, Robert Gates), when they met in Algiers shortly after the revolution. This vision, however, was not shared by Khomeini and the clerics around him. The prospect of normal ties with America alarmed Iran's revolutionaries and prompted them to spring into action.

The stage was set for an all-out battle between the secular and religious forces as each side sought to shape the revolution in its own image. As noted in the previous chapter, numerous institutions and ruling documents were crafted during the pivotal months after the revolution as the foundations of the Islamic Republic were defined. In the realm of foreign policy, Khomeini was appalled by Bazargan's relative moderation, as he detested the United States and relished an opportunity to humiliate the Great Satan. The network of mosques, the Revolutionary Committees, and the vast organizational structure of the clerical militants now went to work agitating against Bazargan and his provisional government. However, Iranian revolutionaries needed a crisis to arouse and rally the population, discredit their foes, and consolidate their power.

Beyond domestic politics, another important motivation for the revolutionaries was to humiliate the United States. Khomeini's defiant message insisted that America was a helpless and weak power. For too long, he believed, many Iranians, including some within the revolutionary coalition, had attributed great power to the United States. Such impressions, if not contradicted, were bound to limit the reach of Iran's revolution. A superpower whose diplomats stood captured and helpless would reinforce Khomeini's slogan that "America cannot do a damn thing." This was an important message of Iranian emancipation at the expense of American pride. The only way to impress his constituents with what he believed to be the fact of American impotence was through manipulating the predicament of its diplomats. The embassy simply proved too irresistible a target for Khomeini.

Since the hostage crisis, there has been a peculiar tendency among Western scholars to absolve Khomeini of responsibility for the actions of the students. It is often claimed that he was not informed beforehand that the militants intended to take over the embassy. The Carter administration based its entire policy of securing the return of the hostages through diplomacy on the notion that the students acted alone and that the task of the United States was to strengthen the moderates who could influence Khomeini in the right direction. Now, almost four decades later, evidence has come to light to suggest that

Khomeini orchestrated the entire affair and hoped that it would help him to consolidate the revolution and solidify Iran's antagonism toward the United States.

In his published memoirs, the late Ayatollah Mohammad-Reza Mahdavi-Kani, a member of the Revolutionary Council and the head of the Revolutionary Committees, offers an intriguing insight into the events surrounding the hostage crisis. Soon after the occupation of the embassy, in his role as the head of the Revolutionary Committees, which were largely responsible for internal security, he contacted Khomeini's son Ahmad, who acted as his father's chief of staff and intermediary with advisors, to inquire about the developments surrounding the embassy.

> The night of the embassy's occupation I contacted Ahmad and asked him what is happening? Initially he just laughed and would not answer. I asked him did you know about this. He laughed. Finally, after I insisted, he said the Imam [Khomeini] is satisfied with this and you should not get involved.[4]

Mahdavi-Kani's pointed questions to Ahmad about his knowledge of the event only elicited bemused laughter, suggesting prior knowledge.

Shortly after the embassy takeover, Bazargan and his government resigned. At the time it appeared that Bazargan, unable to secure the release of the hostages, was swept away by the revolutionary momentum of the day. It is important to stress, however, that the hostage crisis was, for Khomeini, not just about undermining the provisional government, but also

about ensuring that the intellectual foundations of Iran's foreign policy would be radical. Through a symbolic attack on the
US embassy, the new revolutionaries demonstrated not only
their antagonism toward America but also their contempt for
international norms. Khomeini and his cohort understood that
the revolution stood the best chance of surviving and prosper-
ing if Iran was estranged from the West.

None of this was apparent to the Carter administration. At
the outset of the crisis, the White House decided to ensure the
release of the hostages in a manner that did not jeopardize their
physical safety or the possibility of resuming more or less normal diplomatic relations with Iran. An administration that had
perennially misread Iranian politics had no idea that the entire
crisis was instigated by Khomeini himself. Washington still
hoped that private communications and gradual pressure
would quickly end the standoff. The task at hand was to search
for intermediaries to Khomeini and to persuade him to undo
the work of his firebrands. To placate Iranian sensitivities,
Ramsey Clark, President Lyndon Johnson's former attorney
general who had dabbled in left-wing politics and conspiracy
theories, was chosen as an emissary to Tehran. His leftism and
anti-Americanism proved insufficient, as Khomeini refused to
meet all US emissaries.

To avoid antagonizing Iran, the White House chose to pursue a restrained public posture—despite the fact that the hostage seizure had taken place in the midst of Carter's primary
campaign against Senator Ted Kennedy—and offered private
assurances to the Iranians. Washington conveyed to Tehran
that the shah was in America only for medical purposes and
that Iran could confirm this by sending its own physicians to

examine the monarch. The administration also promised Iran that it was free to pursue its claims against the shah's assets in the American court system.

A week after the seizure of the embassy, the Iranian government finally offered its fantastical terms for the release of the captives. The agreement called for the return of the shah and his assets, an apology by the United States for its crimes against the Iranian people, and a pledge of noninterference in Iran's affairs. Given that Khomeini's primary motive was domestic politics and ushering in a radical foreign policy, it is unclear that even the Carter administration's acceptance of these terms would have ended the crisis. As the clerical militants were busy exploiting the events to the detriment of their rivals, they needed to perpetuate the conflict.

The Carter administration now went through some of the processes that a US government could go through when in a tough international spot. It took its case to the International Court of Justice in The Hague and prevailed. It then went to the United Nations Security Council, where a mild resolution was passed calling on Iran to release the hostages. The Soviet Union blocked any imposition of sanctions. The US government then froze Iran's assets. Trade between the two countries came to a halt. Kurt Waldheim, the secretary-general of the United Nations, journeyed to Iran to impress upon the mullahs the importance of these legal measures. He came home empty-handed. The Islamic Republic seemed disdainful of such diplomatic procedures.

The economic pressure imposed on Iran was gradual and designed to incrementally squeeze Tehran into freeing the hostages. The freezing of $12 billion of Iranian assets and the cessation of all bilateral trade had their virtues as pressure tactics. But Iran's economy was already in shambles and the militant republic was more than ready to sever trade ties with the Great Satan. The Islamic Republic was even then looking to Asia and the Soviet bloc as alternative outlets for its needs and exports. Moreover, the immediate postrevolutionary leadership was even less inclined than its successors to make pragmatic cost-benefit assessments.

It is important to note that while the United States condemned Iran's conduct as a breach of international law, it was also a violation of Shiite Islam's own traditions. Historically, Shiite clergy have been generous in assuring safe passage to non-Muslim emissaries. The great Islamic empires were at pains to accommodate diplomats from all countries and treated them with respect and deference. The clerical class, as guardians of the law, had traditionally sanctified these traditions. An entire legal corpus evolved on the need to grant protection to representatives of all states. As a learned Shiite scholar, Khomeini must have known that his conduct contravened the established norms of the Islamic order he was purportedly committed to constructing.

In the one instance during the crisis when Carter took forceful action, his policy actually worked. After the storming of the embassy, there was much loose talk in Tehran about putting the hostages on trial. The administration sent a private note to Iran stressing that any trial would jeopardize Iran's commerce and any harm done to the hostages would provoke American retaliation. Soon, all the talk of a public trial was quietly shelved. This proved to be a lesson not learned, not just by Carter but also by successive American presidents who dealt with Iran. The Islamic Republic does respond to credible threats of force but grows more truculent when offered soothing diplomatic blandishments and offers of dialogue.

Throughout the hostage crisis, Iran used its factional politics to great advantage. President Abolhassan Banisadr and his cagey foreign minister, Sadegh Ghotbzadeh, who dealt with the two French lawyers who served as intermediaries between Washington and Tehran, often spoke of internal rivalries and how moderates were beset by hard-liners. They portrayed themselves as pragmatists fending off the militants in Khomeini's court. An aggressive American policy, they warned, would adversely affect that internal power struggle. And every time Khomeini rebuffed a gesture of compromise, the Parisians would warn their American interlocutors that things could get worse if the United States became more hostile. This proved an effective tactic as US policy sought then, as it has ever since, ways to influence Iran's factional politics.

The evolving position of the United States was to propitiate some of Iran's claims. The Carter White House was prepared to establish a forum whereby Iran would voice its historical grievances against the United States. This policy stipulated that "the United States understood and sympathized with the grievances felt by many Iranian citizens concerning the practices of the previous regime."[5] To that end, the "United States would facilitate any legal action brought by the government of Iran in the courts of the United States to account for assets under the custody or control of the former Shah."[6] This still proved insufficient for Khomeini as he demanded that any public forum be accompanied by an American apology for its crimes. And far from seeking litigation, the Iranians simply demanded the return of the shah's assets at once.

Iranian intransigence and an ineffective sanctions regime made the idea of a rescue mission an appealing option to an increasingly desperate Carter, whose political fortunes were hanging in the balance. The military plan, code-named Operation Eagle Claw, was logistically complicated as it involved flying a contingent of US Army Special Forces to a desert location via helicopter. Once situated, the soldiers would switch to fixed-wing aircraft and proceed toward a location in Tehran. From there, using prepositioned vehicles, they would assault the compound and free the hostages. Even under the best of circumstances, this would be a difficult operation to execute without casualties. The night of April 25, 1980, was hardly a propitious time for launching a military action, as desert sandstorms caused the helicopters to collide with a refueling aircraft, leading to a large explosion and the death of eight American servicemen. Even before the succeeding stages unfolded, the operation was deemed too risky to proceed, and the entire enterprise was aborted. The United States stood utterly humiliated, a superpower that could neither compel Iran to free its diplomats nor mount a credible rescue effort. Suddenly, Khomeini's persistent slogan, "America cannot do a damn thing," appeared eerily true.

The failure of the rescue operation raised the question of whether a more coercive strategy, such as declaring war on Iran or blockading its coast, might have worked. Khomeini launched the hostage takeover partly to consolidate his regime. He might have ended the crisis if he had perceived that it was imperiling the Islamic Republic. Carter, however, always sought a punitive policy that did not jeopardize the prospect of resuming relations with Iran. As with every subsequent president, Carter saw Iran as a collection of factions and hoped to eventually empower the pragmatic moderates. In a time of intense frustration, he did opt for a rescue mission, but that was a circumscribed military operation with the limited goal of freeing the captives and not punishing Iran for its transgressions. To embark on a robust policy would have endangered the prospect of reestablishing ties and undermined the moderates that America sought to empower.

By the fall of 1980, a new factor entered the deliberations over the fate of the hostages: the prospect of a Reagan presidency. As a candidate, Ronald Reagan spoke often about American strength and talked extensively about repairing the post-Vietnam "hollow army" and building up US military capabilities. There was a measure of unpredictability about how Reagan would approach the crisis. This was the point that the Carter administration's own negotiators began making to their Iranian counterparts. Having failed to establish its own credible posture vis-à-vis the Iranians, the Carter White House was now playing the "Reagan card" to strengthen its negotiating hand. Once the Iranians appreciated that the Carter presidency might be coming to a close, they seemed more willing to resolve the crisis.

As Khomeini now looked at the horizon, he felt it was time to end the crisis that had served him so well. The external environment was proving dangerous to Iran. Iraq had invaded

Iran in September 1980 and the hawkish Reagan seemed poised to assume the presidency and usher in an aggressive policy toward the mullahs. In terms of internal politics, Khomeini had successfully purged all the "unreliable" elements from power and imposed a rigid theocracy on a nation that had revolted against the shah in the name of democracy and freedom. This did not mean, however, that Iran would abandon its negotiating terms as the talks dragged on throughout 1980. Khomeini was determined that the hostages would only be set free once Iran had secured many of its demands.

The hostage crisis was finally resolved in January 1981 with the Algiers Accord. At the outset of the crisis, Iran had three distinct demands. First was that the US government acknowledge its crimes against Iran and pledge to refrain henceforth from interfering in its internal politics. In practice, this meant that the United States could never assist democratic forces in Iran. The Algiers Accord went a long way toward granting that Iranian wish when it stipulated "the United States pledges that it is and from now on will be the policy of the United States not to intervene, directly or indirectly, politically or militarily, in Iran's internal affairs."[7] To be sure, there was no American apology for past misdeeds, but this was still a remarkable concession by the Carter administration that bound its successors for years to come, despite the fact that the US government was agreeing to this under duress.

Then there was the Iranian demand that the shah's assets be returned to the Iranian people. The Algiers Accord stipulated that "the United States will freeze, and prohibit any transfer of, property and assets in the United States within the control of the estate of the former Shah or of any close relative of the former Shah served as a defendant in U.S. litigation brought by Iran to recover such property and assets as belonging to Iran."[8] This was not an immediate repatriation of the shah's assets, but it did go a long way to accommodate Iran's demands against one of America's oldest and most reliable allies.

The question of economic sanctions was quickly set aside. The United States maintained its bilateral measures but did not insist that the rest of the world follow suit. Soon, international commerce returned to Iran, led by America's own European and Asian allies. The Islamic Republic, with its distrust of the international system, did not seem an easy place to do business, but it still managed to secure contracts and sell its oil.

The hostage crisis ended in an agreement that was a compromise document. The Islamic Republic did not pay a price for its egregious breach of international law and diplomatic norms and its humiliation of the United States. In the end, it extracted a commitment from the United States not to assist any democratic protest movements in Iran as this would constitute meddling in its internal affairs. The agreement went on to make the shah's assets vulnerable to legal seizure by a regime with no respect for international law. There were also no lingering economic costs for Iran's seizure of the embassy. In its first diplomatic encounter with the United States, the Islamic Republic clearly came out on top.

IRAN-CONTRA AFFAIR

The resolution of the hostage crisis ushered in a more forward-leaning American policy in the Middle East. The hawkish

Reagan administration embraced a policy of coercion and containment of Iran. The United States tilted toward Iraq in its war against Iran, providing Baghdad with agricultural credits and, even more importantly, intelligence. The centrality of the Middle East to America's security concerns meant that the United States was not about to abandon the region to Iran's ideological enterprise. Indeed, the more mischievous Iran became, the more Washington grew determined to sustain its allies and bolster its presence. Given the Reagan White House's pronounced hostility to the clerical regime, the decision to trade arms for American hostages held in Lebanon in the mid-1980s seems unusual. But it was a recurrence of the same assumptions that had guided the Carter administration, namely that the United States could affect Iran's factional politics by subtle use of incentives.

The tale of the Iran-Contra affair goes back to the tribulations of Lebanon in the early 1980s. In June 1982, Israel took advantage of the chaos of the long-simmering civil war to invade Lebanon in the hope of evicting the Palestine Liberation Organization (PLO) from its latest sanctuary and installing a more docile government. The first goal was achieved with ease, but imposing a friendly regime next door eluded Israel. The US-brokered arrival of multinational forces to supervise the PLO's departure led to the dispatch of American peacekeepers to Lebanon.

Iran's Hezbollah proxy now went to work and began a systematic assault on the US presence in Lebanon. On April 18, 1983, a Hezbollah truck bomb exploded outside the US embassy in Beirut, killing sixty-three people, among them seventeen

Americans, including Robert Ames, the Central Intelligence Agency's national intelligence officer for the Middle East. On October 23, 1983, in one of the most spectacular uses of suicide bombing in the Middle East, Hezbollah attacked the US Marine Corps barracks near Beirut International Airport, killing 241 soldiers. It was the largest loss of American lives to terrorism before the 9/11 attacks in 2001. Soon, American academics, clergymen, journalists, and even intelligence officials were caught up in the whirlwind. Hostage-taking became Hezbollah's latest tactic. It was at this point that Israel and Iran began their peculiar relationship that would soon involve the United States.

As the war with Iraq dragged on, the Iranian military desperately needed spare parts for its American-supplied legacy armaments. The Reagan administration's Operation Staunch had successfully closed off many avenues for Iran to obtain either American or European weapons. Soon after the war began, Israel had quietly started supplying Iran with arms. For the Israelis at that time, Iraq represented a greater threat than Iran. Saddam was busy developing his nuclear program, openly decrying the Camp David peace accords, and vying to lead the Arab world against Israel. The Jewish state had no love for the Iranian theocracy, but appreciated that its defeat would only embolden Iraq. Thus, the Israelis were happy to sell arms to Iran. The only problem was that Israel could not transfer certain categories of weapons to Iran without US permission. Thus began America's entanglement in the arms-for-hostages deal.

By this time, a confluence of factors beyond Israeli lobbying began to make the idea of a new approach to Iran attractive to many in Washington. Some within the US bureaucracy were growing concerned that Iran's isolation could only benefit the Soviet Union in the Middle East. A beleaguered Iran in search of allies might just reach out to Russia and gradually come under Soviet influence. For many officials within the CIA and the National Security Council (NSC), it was time for a diplomatic opening to Tehran. Moreover, in Iran's persistent factionalism, they saw hope for a policy that could strengthen the moderate elements. Some within the CIA, as part of this outreach effort, even recommended arms sales. The Reagan administration hoped to use the levers of diplomacy to alter Iran's internal balance of power, which in turn would lead to a shift in Iran's foreign policy. This would not be the first or the last administration that sought to condition the politics of a country that it poorly understood.

The Soviet-centric view found a hospitable home in the White House, which regarded most regional issues within the Cold War context. The trusted William Casey, CIA director and the president's former campaign manager, insisted that the United States could not allow Iran to collapse behind the Iron Curtain. The Russian occupation of Afghanistan, which both Washington and Tehran opposed, was seen as an example of geopolitical common ground that could be enhanced through dialogue and cooperation. It was time for Iran to come in from the cold.

Beyond the geopolitical and strategic arguments, the plight of the American hostages held in Lebanon weighed heavily on Reagan. As with Carter, Reagan found himself preoccupied with the fate of hostages, whose release continued to elude his administration. The humanitarian claims were particularly acute in the case of one hostage, William Buckley, the CIA station chief in Beirut, whose condition was considered worrisome given the harsh conditions and brutal torture to which he was subjected. The ordeal of the captured Americans led Reagan to press his intelligence services and the State Department to produce results. The president wanted the hostages out, the CIA wanted to prevent Iran's absorption into the Soviet zone, and the entire US government wanted to empower the so-called moderates in Iran.

Were there moderates in Iran willing to normalize relations with the United States if only they obtained a cache of arms? To be sure, the Islamic Republic had factions and divisions of opinion on foreign policy issues, as does every country. The more pragmatic politicians such as the late speaker of the parliament, Ali Akbar Hashemi Rafsanjani, sensed that Iran could not remain entirely isolated from the West. The exigencies of the war demanded a source of arms to rebuff the more advanced Iraqi army. This was pragmatism born out of necessity, as Iran could not wage war or deal with its economic burdens from a position of total isolation. It would be a misreading of the domestic situation, however, to suggest that such a pragmatic redefinition of interests constituted a fundamental reorientation of the regime.

The many US officials who endorsed the idea of the theocratic moderates also failed to appreciate that Khomeini was still the central actor in Iran's decision-making process. For Khomeini to achieve his goal of toppling Saddam, his forces required weapons that only the United States could provide.

Thus, his willingness to trade arms for hostages was not so much a desire to begin a new relationship with the United States as an appreciation that his maximalist war aims necessitated some adjustments. For Khomeini, America still remained the Great Satan, but one with an arsenal that could be used instrumentally against the more immediate danger of Saddam. In the end, it was not the rise of moderates so much as the requirements of a desperate regime waging a costly war that governed Tehran's approach to the arms deal.

Still, it was at this point that the United States joined the back channel to Iran established by the Israelis. As the transaction unfolded, many within the US bureaucracy were left in the dark. Former National Security Advisor Robert "Bud" McFarlane, aided by NSC staffer Colonel Oliver North, was largely in charge. As the Iran gambit unfolded, North was looking for ways to assist the Nicaraguan rebels, the Contras, who were battling the Sandinista government in Managua. Indeed, the attempt to resist and roll back communist gains in Latin America had become one of the central pillars of the Reagan doctrine, an effort to use resistance to socialist governments installed with Moscow's assistance to inflict damage on the Soviet Union. The struggle to sustain the Contras in Nicaragua after Congress cut off their funding was among the most important objectives of the Reagan administration. Soon, American military equipment began flowing into Iran and a number of hostages were occasionally released. In an even more bizarre development, the proceeds from the arms sales were diverted to the Contras—in contravention of congressional prohibitions of US government-appropriated funds being used to support the Nicaraguan rebels.

On May 25, 1986, McFarlane, North, and four other officials were finally presented with an opportunity to embark on a historic journey. The American emissaries had come bearing gifts, including a Bible signed by Reagan and a chocolate cake in the shape of a key. The former national security advisor and his entourage landed in Tehran hoping to meet then President Ali Khamenei and Speaker Rafsanjani, but instead they were relegated to meeting second-tier officials. McFarlane had come prepared to discuss means of ending the Iran-Iraq War, restoring relations between the United States and Iran, and securing the freedom of American hostages held in Lebanon. The Iranians just wanted to discuss a secure and steady channel for obtaining arms and were prepared to dangle the prospective release of the hostages to entice the Americans. Iran was not seeking a transformation of relations but a transaction involving arms and hostages. In the end, although some hostages were released, more were captured. Americans in Lebanon became a prized commodity of exchange for Iran.

The inevitable revelation of the plot, involving arms sales to an adversary and transfer of the profits from those sales to the Contras, rocked the Reagan administration. The Iran-Contra affair inflicted significant damage on the credibility and standing of Reagan's presidency. The final congressional report issued a scathing indictment of the whole affair: "The Iran initiative succeeded only in replacing three American hostages with another three, arming Iran with 2,004 TOWs [tube-launched, optically tracking, wire-guided missiles] and more than 200 vital spare parts for HAWK missile batteries, improperly generating funds for the Contras and other covert activities."[9] Several Reagan administration officials were indicted or forced to accept plea deals as a result of the revelations. Others were threatened with indictments for years as the special prosecutor's interminable investigation continued, inevitably bleeding over into the criminalization of policy differences.

The Iran-Contra affair remains an illustration of the pitfalls and difficulties of dealing with Iran. A number of factors bedeviled the initiative. The administration's poor understanding of Iranian politics and Khomeini's animosity toward the United States made a breakthrough virtually impossible. The most glaring assumption of the entire initiative was the notion that moderate elements would use the arms deal to displace their radical rivals. For the Iranians, the entire affair was not a grand gesture of reconciliation with the United States but a commercial arrangement designed to secure much-needed military equipment. Tehran would likely have played the game of trading arms for hostages much longer had the entire affair not been revealed. In the end, it is unlikely that the initiative would have lasted as the United States ultimately could not sustain a policy of paying ransom for its citizens under the guise of diplomatic outreach.

The Iran-Contra affair damaged Reagan's presidency and blemished his legacy. The administration spent the remainder of its time in office trying to repair America's Arab alliances, which were severely strained by the secret US diplomatic effort. Saudi Arabia went so far as to clandestinely acquire Chinese ballistic missiles in part to send a message of displeasure to Washington. However, the one aspect of the Iran-Contra affair that did survive the debacle was the notion that US diplomacy can condition Iran's factional politics. The flawed logic that Reagan had inherited from Carter survived its most devastating test.

During the Reagan years, the Islamic Republic continued to effectively advance its goals with impunity. Iran created Hezbollah and then used its proxy to perpetrate one of the worst terrorist attacks in American history. Tehran followed this up by commanding Hezbollah to take Americans hostage. Far from paying a price for its transgressions, Iran saw America come calling with a diplomatic channel that traded hostages for much-needed arms. Once more, the Islamic Republic used its factional politics to shield itself from retribution and extract concessions from America. Washington feared that using force against Iran would empower the hard-liners, while offering it arms would somehow enable its moderates. Although many have tried, no country has ever used its factional politics to better effect.

GEORGE W. BUSH: THE DIPLOMATIST

The terrorist attacks on New York and Washington on September 11, 2001, were a defining moment in recent US history. For decades, successive administrations had relied on repressive and unrepresentative governments in the region to provide stability. Academic students of the Arab world and many practitioners had concluded that the regional order was durable since the regimes had mastered the instruments of repression that enabled them to maintain a monopoly on power. In effect, experts pronounced the regimes to be "coup-proof." American policy-makers did not pay much attention to the religious extremism that was corroding the Arab order or its decaying institutions. George W. Bush, who had hoped that his presidency would focus on domestic problems and avoid the humanitarian interventions and nation-building efforts that had marked the Clinton administration's years in office, now had to confront the Middle East with all its pathologies and resentments.

The public reaction in Iran to the 9/11 attacks was a spontaneous outburst of pro-American sentiment rather than the demonstrations in support of the attacks that occurred in most of the Arab countries and Pakistan. In some ways, these manifestations were symptomatic of public disaffection with the clerical regime. At the same time, the 9/11 Commission, led by Lee Hamilton and Thomas Kean, found strong evidence of links between the Iranian government and al-Qaeda, including the facilitation of travel of al-Qaeda members who were part of the hijack team, a pattern that continues to this day despite the alleged incompatibility of Sunni- and Shiite-based versions of Islamism. The Iranian government itself reflected this Janus-like reaction to the United States when it was confronted by the initial US military response to 9/11—the invasion of Afghanistan and the overthrow of the Taliban regime there that had hosted the al-Qaeda terrorists responsible for the attacks.

Enmity against the Taliban regime appeared to provide the United States and Iran with an overlapping, common interest in the future of Afghanistan. As Afghanistan descended into protracted civil war in the 1990s after the Soviet withdrawal, the United States retreated from involvement there since it could discern no compelling national interest at stake. Iran, for its part, increasingly became the leading patron of Ahmad Shah Massoud's Northern Alliance, which represented the last bastion of organized opposition to the emerging Taliban movement and was made up of young foot soldiers schooled in Sunni-extremist madrassas in Pakistan. This patronage led to a confrontation between the Iranian regime and the Taliban in 1998 after a number of Iranian citizens were kidnapped and eight Iranian diplomats were murdered by Afghans in Mazar-e-Sharif. Tehran mobilized seventy thousand troops on the Afghan border in a show of force before tensions were eased by a United Nations mediation effort that led to the release of the remaining hostages.

The United States, having "walked away" from Afghanistan, to use Secretary of Defense Robert Gates's phrase, had few tools at its disposal with which to eliminate the Taliban regime after the 9/11 attacks. Leaders of the Northern Alliance, with whom the CIA had maintained contact after the 1992 collapse of the Afghan Communist regime, commanded the only organized military force and were virtually the only tool available to the United States.[10] Soon, CIA officers and US special operations forces established contact with the Northern Alliance and provided it with air cover that allowed it to drive the Taliban from

Mazar-e-Sharif and other Afghan cities, ultimately pushing the Taliban and its al-Qaeda allies out of the country and into Pakistan. This was all done with the acquiescence, if not tacit approval, of Tehran. When the United States attempted to then put together a functioning Afghan government at the Bonn conference in the late fall of 2001, Iranian diplomats were present and consulting with their US counterparts.

Ambassador James Dobbins was an American diplomat with extensive experience in post-conflict stabilization efforts in Haiti, Bosnia, and Kosovo. He headed the US delegation and had a strong bias in favor of working with regional powers as a key element in stabilizing Afghanistan. Dobbins was assisted by NSC Senior Director Zalmay Khalilzad, an Afghan-American academic who had previous experience as the Pentagon's assistant deputy undersecretary for policy planning. He would later become ambassador to Afghanistan and Iraq. He too believed that the Iranians would be needed to stabilize Afghanistan. Both diplomats described their conversations with then Iranian deputy foreign minister Muhammad Javad Zarif and Mohammad Taherian (who had served as the Iranian link to the Northern Alliance and would become ambassador to Kabul) as constructive and, indeed, crucial at key moments in persuading the Afghans to accept a broad and inclusive government headed by the Pashtun leader Hamid Karzai.

Although the formal state apparatus, via the Ministry of Foreign Affairs, was content to make constructive contributions to the Bonn talks, a steady stream of reports suggested that other elements of the Iranian state were taking steps to destabilize Afghanistan. Specifically, the Revolutionary Guards were providing small arms and other weaponry to the Taliban, allegedly including explosively formed penetrators (EFPs) used in roadside bombs that were capable of inflicting serious casualties on US and NATO forces. The pattern became so persistent that, by 2007, Undersecretary of State Nicholas Burns angrily noted that there was "irrefutable evidence" that the government of the Islamic Republic was responsible for the provision of these weapons.[11]

The cooperative approach of Iranian diplomats in Afghanistan was undermined not only by the Revolutionary Guards' activities there but also by their efforts at subversion and support for terrorism in the broader Middle East. Early in 2002, the Israelis intercepted a ship, the *Karine A*, that was loaded with weapons intended for Palestinian terror groups in the West Bank and the Gaza Strip. Hezbollah—whose then terror operations chief, the late Imad Mughniyeh, had masterminded the assault on the US Marine barracks in Beirut in 1983 and the murder of US Navy diver Robert Stethem in 1986—appears to have brokered the deal. For this and other reasons, including continued suspicions about Iran's pursuit of nuclear weapons capabilities, Bush labeled Iran as part of an "axis of evil" in his State of the Union address in January 2002.

In the early months of 2003, Khalilzad and Zarif maintained desultory contacts when the latter became Iran's ambassador to the United Nations in order to discuss the future of Iraq, to which the US government was now turning its attention. Iraq was another Iranian neighbor whose policies might have appeared to create a confluence of US and Iranian interests. Khalilzad, who was accompanied by State Department diplomat

Ryan Crocker, explained that the United States intended to eliminate the Baath regime, eliminate Iraq's capability for weapons of mass destruction, and put in place a pluralistic, democratic regime at peace with its neighbors. According to Khalilzad's account, "The important point here was unsaid: the United States, contrary to public accusations from Iran's supreme leader, Ayatollah Khamenei, had no plans to expand the war into Iran." In fact, rather than confrontation, the United States sought Iranian cooperation with regard to overflights and Iranian influence on the Iraqi Shiite community. Although the Iranians opposed a US invasion, they readily agreed to cooperate to de-escalate the military activities.[12]

After the fall of Saddam, the discussions turned to terrorism and the negotiations became stickier. The Iranians demanded that the United States turn over the leaders of the Mojahedin-e-Khalq (MEK), which had been opposing the Iranian regime from Iraq since shortly after the overthrow of the shah. During the Clinton years, the MEK had been added to the Foreign Terrorist Organizations list as a sop to the Islamic Republic in an effort to jump-start the "road map" to normalization between Washington and Tehran. Now, however, its members were protected persons under a US occupation. Khalilzad told Zarif that although the United States would "disarm" the MEK, it would not turn over the leaders to the Iranians. The United States, for its part, was interested in al-Qaeda operatives who were thought to be under house arrest in Iran. The Iranians, despite some hints that they might be interested in an exchange of MEK members for al-Qaeda terrorists, were generally nonresponsive. Khalilzad observed that within days of his meeting with Zarif, a truck bomb blew up at a Saudi Arabian housing complex, killing eight Americans. When that bomb was connected to al-Qaeda fanatics in Iran, the Bush administration decided to cut off negotiations with the Iranians.

This led to one of the more perplexing episodes in US-Iranian diplomacy, one that continues to condition innumerable conspiracy theories. This is the story of the alleged Iranian offer in 2003 to negotiate with the United States. A key perpetrator of this hoax was the senior Swiss diplomat, Ambassador Tim Guldimann, in Tehran. The Swiss had been serving as the "protecting power" for US interests in Iran since the breakdown of relations in 1979. As a result, all official messages between the two governments were passed through the so-called Swiss channel. Guldimann was an activist by nature and harbored ambitions to be more than a hollow log through which messages between Tehran and Washington could be passed. He hoped to spark a rapprochement between the United States and Iran. Weeks after 9/11, Guldimann traveled to Washington to promote the idea. He returned in May 2003, purporting to carry a letter from the Iranians proposing comprehensive negotiations on the nuclear program, terrorism, and Iran's regional activities. The actual provenance of the letter has been disputed. Many Iran apologists have tirelessly spread the story that this was a serious offer of negotiations quashed by Vice President Dick Cheney, Secretary of Defense Donald Rumsfeld, and National Security Advisor Condoleezza Rice. Rice denies seeing it, as do Cheney and Rumsfeld. In fact, senior State Department officials have said repeatedly that they believed the letter was the work of Guldimann and the Iranian ambassador in France, Sadeq Kharazi, the nephew of the Iranian foreign minister, and that in light of conditions at the time, it was not worth pursuing. Published versions of the document also make clear that the Iranians were demanding a US blessing for Iranian access to the full nuclear fuel cycle as a prerequisite for the talks, something that would come later in the Obama administration. The pause in US-Iranian direct negotiations would continue for four years.

By this time, however, a new crisis loomed over Iran, namely its nuclear ambitions. The Islamic Republic had maintained a nuclear program since its assumption of power in 1979. The clerical leaders were as attracted to the power of atomic arms as their monarch predecessor. However, in 2002, what was once considered a manageable situation became a full-blown crisis. The first shock came when an opposition group announced that Iran had constructed an elaborate enrichment facility in Natanz, approximately two hundred miles south of Tehran. The complex procedure of enriching uranium was once thought to be beyond Iran's technological capacity. In addition, Iran was active in developing its plutonium capabilities. The uranium conversion facility in Isfahan and the nearly completed heavy-water reactor and production plant in Arak demonstrated a diversified path to nuclear empowerment. The scope of the program showed that Iran had developed an elaborate nuclear infrastructure and had successfully concealed it from the International Atomic Energy Agency (IAEA).

The Iranian reformist government led by President Mohammad Khatami immediately recognized that it had a serious problem on its hands. The revelations had come at a time when America was in the midst of "shock and awe" confidence in the wake of its rapid displacement of the Taliban in Afghanistan and on the cusp of its destruction of the Baathist regime of Saddam Hussein in a mere three weeks. As we have seen, the latter truly staggered the Iranian political establishment, which had been assured by its military leaders that America could not discharge that task with such ease and speed. The fear in Iran was that America would next turn its gaze on the Islamic Republic. After all, no regime represented the nexus between terrorism and weapons of mass destruction—the criteria for inclusion in the "axis of evil"—the way that Iran did. It was time for the clerical state to buy time and wait for the storm to pass.

The Europeans appeared eager to engage with Iran and establish themselves as prime interlocutors since their focus at this time was more on limiting American power than on restraining Iranian ambitions. The revelations by an Iranian opposition group of undeclared Iranian nuclear activity at Natanz and Arak galvanized European capitals, where fear of US unilateral action against Iran was palpable. Responding to this intelligence, the IAEA Board of Governors passed a resolution in the fall of 2003 calling for Iran to freeze its nuclear enrichment and reprocessing activities and declare all of its nuclear facilities and materials to the IAEA. Fearing a crisis between the United States and Iran on the heels of the invasion of Iraq, diplomats from the United Kingdom, France, and Germany (eventually joined by Francisco Javier Solana, former NATO secretary-general and subsequently a European Union high commissioner) interceded to negotiate with the Iranians, despite US misgivings. The negotiations succeeded in getting Iran to commit to freezing its nuclear activities, making a full declaration to the IAEA, and allowing further inspections under the Additional Protocol to the Non-Proliferation Treaty (NPT). The European Union, for its part, would provide technical assistance in building a light-water reactor (believed to be more proliferation-proof than heavy-water reactors) and procuring nuclear fuel as well as pursuing negotiations on a trade agreement and support for Iranian accession to the World Trade Organization. This effort to bribe the Iranians out of their nuclear program bore eerie echoes of an earlier US effort to do the same with North Korea. The irony was that the so-called Agreed Framework with North Korea was being exposed as totally deficient at precisely the same time that the European Union was attempting to replicate it with Iran. North Korean officials, confronted by their US interlocutors with evidence that North Korea was clandestinely pursuing uranium enrichment capability, admitted their duplicity after foreswearing the plutonium path to the bomb. The negotiating process with North Korea wobbled on for six more years before collapsing in recriminations and nuclear tests in 2009.

The European Union-led negotiating effort with Iran over the next two years was largely a diplomatic game of cat and mouse, much as Bush administration officials had feared. Iran failed to come clean with the IAEA but complained bitterly that it had not received the promised technical assistance from the EU. Eventually, Iran's nuclear negotiator, President Hassan

Rouhani, would admit in interviews and his own book that the Iranians used the negotiating process with the EU as a convenient interlude during which they could escape pressure from the international community and rectify some technical glitches that were plaguing their enrichment program.

By 2005, both America's fortunes and Iran's politics began to change. The United States' failure to pacify Iraq and the developing sectarian civil war sapped American power, undermining the once-lofty ambitions of transforming Arab politics that Bush had articulated at the outset of Operation Iraqi Freedom. As Iraq drained the United States, America's adversaries began reconsidering their options. The Islamic Republic, once frightened of the United States, began reviving its ambitions. And no one was more adept at mocking American power than its new president, Mahmoud Ahmadinejad.

Ahmadinejad began as a long-shot candidate for the presidency against the better-known Ali Akbar Hashemi Rafsanjani, a former president and parliamentary speaker. But he had one important ace in the hole: the quiet but unmistakable support of the supreme leader. Throughout his campaign for the presidency, Ahmadinejad made clear his contempt for Iran's subtle nuclear policy. He continually derided Iran's negotiating team and denounced the reformers as too easily capitulating to Western imperialism. As an advocate of confrontational policy, he insisted that Iran could gain more by being aggressive. As one of his first acts in office, Ahmadinejad ended the suspension of the uranium enrichment program and Iran resumed its nuclear activities. Echoing Khomeini's slogan, he insisted that "America cannot do a damn thing."[13]

In its second term, the Bush administration seemed ready to turn the page. Under the leadership of the new secretary of state, Condoleezza Rice, the United States sought to rehabilitate European alliances that had frayed over disagreements about the Iraq War. Washington was also faced with growing pressure from an alarmed Israel about the technological pace of the Iranian nuclear effort. The Europeans wanted the Americans to be involved in the talks with Iran, and a secretary of state who prized diplomacy and alliance-management heeded their call. Thus began the Bush administration's two-track policy toward Iran that would prove to be Rice's most enduring legacy. The policy would guide both the Bush and Obama administrations.

In essence, the two-track policy sought to exert pressure on Iran by isolating it internationally while stressing its economy. This effort was in service of a second diplomatic track to find a way to end Iran's nuclear program via negotiation rather than forcible regime-change, as had been the case in Iraq. The venue of the negotiations now moved to the IAEA Board of Governors and ultimately to the United Nations Security Council (to which the IAEA referred the Iranian nuclear file). The Iran issue became the purview of the so-called P5+1, which consisted of the five permanent members of the UN Security Council (the United States, Russia, China, the United Kingdom, and France) plus Germany. Washington engineered a series of unanimous Security Council resolutions that called on Iran to suspend its uranium enrichment program. The task at hand was to confront Iran with international unity and to demonstrate to the mullahs that even Russia and China were concerned about their nuclear ambitions.

The US bureaucracy that proved to be the most imaginative and creative at this stage of the negotiating process was, by far, the Department of the Treasury. Using the Security Council resolution's legal authority, Treasury officials, especially Under Secretary Stuart Levey, began pressing global financial institutions to curtail their transactions with Iran. The name-and-shame campaign led Treasury officials to journey across the world and describe in lurid detail the potential reputational damage to banks that were dealing with a regime censured by the United Nations for its nuclear proliferation as well as its support for international terrorism and other illicit activities. The campaign was slow but steady. Eventually, Iran started to feel the squeeze as financial institutions began to spurn its business out of fear that they would be denied access to the US financial system. Suddenly, Iran found it difficult to process its oil deals, with the proceeds of its sales lingering in banks abroad.

The two-track policy was not just about pressure, as the P5+1 members were also ready to negotiate with Iran. For its part, the Bush administration was not prepared to abandon all of its previous conditions for negotiations: it still insisted that it would not participate directly in the talks until Iran once more suspended its uranium enrichment program. After all, this was the demand of the Security Council resolutions, and their fulfillment was the precondition of American participation in the talks—a precondition that Iran never accepted.

Throughout this period, Iran's nuclear program surged ahead. The Islamic Republic installed more and more centrifuges, sought to develop advanced versions, and secretly started constructing another enrichment facility in the mountains near the shrine city of Qom. Iran rejected various offers from the P5+1, dissembled about its previous activities in nuclear military research, and continuously developed an arsenal of ballistic missiles whose only conceivable military purpose was delivering a nuclear payload.

As the negotiations deadlocked, it was Washington that came under increasing pressure to adjust its red lines. The notion that Iran should suspend its uranium enrichment program before US officials joined the talks came under blistering attacks from the Democratic Party. European allies would also intimate privately that the suspension was no longer tenable. Everyone was looking for a way of jump-starting the talks, and the notion that if only American diplomats were at the table all would be well seemed to gain significant traction in public debate. By July 2008, the Bush administration eased its own standards. A US representative, Under Secretary of State William J. Burns, was allowed to observe the talks, although he was not a formal participant. Had the Bush administration not run out of time, it is likely it would have been pressured to offer even more concessions. The Iranians have long managed to gain concessions from their negotiating counterparts by simply showing up to the talks. They were once more poised to play the same old trick that had served them so well in the past.

Throughout the Bush years, the United States focused on crafting economic sanctions and establishing an international consensus on Iran's nuclear program. But it did not clearly define what it considered an acceptable outcome. Was the United States prepared to recognize Iran's right to enrich uranium, as Tehran demanded? Was Washington ready to concede that Iran can be treated as any other member of the NPT, irrespective of its past infractions and continued support for terrorism? The Bush team appeared to envision success as Iran having a very limited and symbolic program that could not be misused for military purposes. By failing to clearly articulate its terms, however, it left open the possibility that whatever standards it had in mind would become attenuated as the negotiations dragged on.

As these developments played out, US-Iranian relations over Iraq deteriorated badly. The superficial confluence of interests in seeing Saddam Hussein removed from the scene gave way to an increasingly naked bid for power by Iran and its proxy militias inside Iraq. Networks of Iranian agents provided Shiite insurgents with extremely deadly capabilities like the EFPs mentioned above, which killed and maimed scores of US servicemen who were trying desperately to fight off former regime elements and the Sunni extremists of al-Qaeda in Iraq amid the sectarian violence of Iran's clients. The latter included terrorists trained by Hezbollah, who were wreaking havoc on Iraqi society. US Army Special Forces devoted particular attention to Iranian agent networks that were providing the EFPs to cell-based paramilitary organizations known as the "special groups." Although some in the Bush administration advocated a harder line on Iran—publicizing Iranian support for violence and ethnic cleansing and designating members of the Quds

Force as enemy combatants—officials on the ground and a majority of the senior officials in Washington believed that negotiations with Iran might prove more effective in combating the most extreme manifestations of Iranian behavior.

The close attention of US Special Forces to the Iranians and the detention of some of their agents and surrogates did attract Tehran's notice. At the end of 2006, the Iranians signaled a desire to talk with Ryan Crocker, the US ambassador to Iraq, who led the effort for negotiations with the Iranians that began in May 2007. The discussions were brokered in part by Iraqi Prime Minister Nouri al-Maliki, a Shiite politician who had spent twenty years of exile in Syria and was heavily influenced by Tehran. Crocker's counterparts, unlike those in his earlier discussions with Iranians over Afghanistan in 2002, were not diplomats but Revolutionary Guard functionaries. The desultory talks dragged on for a few months but yielded no visible results. Eventually, the Iranians overplayed their hand. Internecine fighting among Shiite groups broke out, and even al-Maliki, fed up with the violence sown by Iran, now saw the Iranian special groups as a threat. He ordered the March 2008 "Charge of the Knights" to cut the Iranian proxies down to size. Rather impetuously, he ordered Iraqi security forces to Basra to clean out the Shiite militias who were running roughshod in the city. British military officials had earlier bragged about their "light touch" approach toward counterinsurgency, learned through the hard experience of dealing with Northern Ireland's "troubles" from 1969 to1998. But by 2008 they had conceded failure in stabilizing Basra, which had been their mission after the 2003 invasion of Iraq. British forces concluded Basra was ungovernable and abandoned the city center. Al-Maliki's unanticipated military operation forced US Commanding General David Petraeus's hand. Marine Major General George Flynn was hastily dispatched to Basra to provide the command-and-control and planning elements that turned al-Maliki's improvisational military action into a striking success for the government and a major setback for Iran's clients. This did not end Iran's meddling in Iraq, but it did show the results of a more muscular policy.

Iran fared reasonably well during the post-9/11 years. A regime committed to terrorism that was developing a clandestine nuclear program ended up in a negotiating process with the great powers. Iran proved defiant in the talks as it violated successive United Nations resolutions calling on it to suspend its program with seeming impunity. In the meantime, Iran continued to consolidate its power and influence in Afghanistan and Iraq, while challenging American forces in both countries. The Islamic Republic came out of the Bush years with its nuclear program intact and its regional ambitions enlarged.

Despite the conventional wisdom that the Bush administration had rejected diplomacy with a charter member of the "axis of evil," throughout the eight years of Bush's tenure the United States and Iran engaged in intense (albeit at times indirect) diplomacy. The Islamic Republic managed to reach many of its objectives, even when holding talks with an American government that was hostile to its ambitions. To be sure, Iran did participate in a series of conferences to bring forth a new Afghan government. However, this was mostly driven by self-interest as Iran ensured that the transition process in Afghanistan did not jeopardize its essential interests. Iran preferred to see a non-Taliban regime in Kabul, but was also quite willing to supply the Taliban with lethal military assistance. This served the purpose of hastening America's ultimate withdrawal from a neighboring country, while also serving as a hedge in the event of a Taliban return to power.

The Islamic Republic refused a similar offer from the Americans to help assure a transition process in Iraq as it was too busy deepening that hapless country's sectarian cleavages. In the meantime, Iran unleashed its lethal Shiite militias against the United States military to great effect. While the United States was facing its darkest days dealing with a worsening insurgency in Iraq, the renewed multilateral nuclear negotiations were launched in a format that was destined to work against the United States as the negotiations predictably dragged on. The more the talks appeared to be stalemated, the more the Russians and Chinese, as well as the Europeans, would insist on American concessions to salvage the process. Altogether this constituted a virtuoso record for an Iranian government that, in the immediate aftermath of 9/11 and the United States' vigorous response in Afghanistan and Iraq, was in fear of its life.

OBAMA'S OUTREACH

Barack Obama came into office determined to engage the Islamic Republic. He campaigned as an opponent of "stupid wars" and an advocate for unconditional outreach to American adversaries—including Iran. The new president stressed in his maiden foreign policy speech in Cairo that Iran had a "right to access peaceful nuclear energy" and offered talks "without precondition."[14] The Bush administration's policy of not participating in the talks unless Tehran first suspended its program was forfeited. Iran obtained a critical concession from the United States without having done anything other than continue its nuclear activities at full tilt. The lesson to Tehran was clear: intransigence could be an effective negotiating technique. It would successfully apply that lesson over the eight years of the Obama administration. As it turned out, dropping the demand for suspension of enrichment was just the first of a cascade of concessions that the Obama White House would make to Iran. As a result, the final agreement that the P5+1 negotiated, the Joint Comprehensive Plan of Action, stands as the most deficient arms control agreement in American history.

Obama would prove to be the architect of his own Iran policy, if not his own unusual strategic doctrine. At its core, the Obama presidency was about propitiating US enemies who, in the mind of the president, had been wronged historically by the American imperium. In the Obama cosmology, Iranian clerics, Cuban communists, and Chinese chauvinists are all victims of centuries of American and Western abuse and exploitation. No agreement with them should demand reciprocity, since they are the disadvantaged parties and America is the superpower. In this view, diplomacy cannot be detached from the expiation of past wrongs.

As the Obama White House plotted its strategy, the Islamic Republic went through one of the most consequential political crises in its history. The presidential election of 2009 featured an array of lackluster candidates who seemed destined to be forgotten. For decades, Supreme Leader Ali Khamenei had consolidated his authority by vesting control of governing institutions in his young followers. Ahmadinejad was clearly Khamenei's choice in the summer of 2009 and the muscle of the state was behind his reelection. Nonetheless, former prime minister Mir-Hossein Mousavi, who had been out of office since 1989, managed to capture the national imagination. His stinging critique of Ahmadinejad's incompetence and bellicosity resonated with the public. By all appearances, Mousavi won the majority of votes on Election Day.

In an ominous break from tradition, moments after the polls closed, Iran's official organs began declaring Ahmadinejad the victor by an impressive twenty-three-point margin. In a coordinated campaign, the media outlets quickly followed suit and celebrated the incumbent's landslide. The morning after the election, Khamenei hailed the vote as a "divine assessment" and warned the opposition against "provocative behavior." The regime must have thought that warnings and displays of power would overcome the crisis of a transparently contrived election result. Yet the guardians of the revolution badly miscalculated the mood of their citizenry. The ensuing street protests, the largest since the fall of the shah in 1979, were repressed at great human cost and took an incalculable toll on the legitimacy of the regime.

The turmoil in Iran provided Obama's cool realism and commitment to unconditional engagement with its first crisis. Soon after coming to power, the American president had penned a letter to the supreme leader expressing his desire for a respect-ful dialogue. Through Oman, the administration was in the process of establishing a back channel to Iran. The stage had seemed set for the long-awaited dialogue between the two nations, until the Iranian people revolted against their govern-ment. It was at this point that the White House made the fateful decision not to support the Iranian people seeking to reclaim their stolen votes. President Obama remained largely silent and the White House issued bland statements expressing concern about violence. The CIA was enjoined against any attempt to support the Green rebellion. In the summer of 2009, Washington opted for preserving its back channel to the Islamist regime and turned a blind eye to the Green Move-ment's struggle for freedom, even as Iranian citizens chanted "Obama, are you with us or against us?" It was an important lost opportunity to turn the internal cleavages inside Iran into an instrument of pressure to get Iran to change course.

It must be stressed that, contrary to the accepted wisdom of the Obama administration, the disturbances of that summer posed a serious threat to the Islamist order. In a speech in 2013, Khamenei admitted that the Green Movement brought the regime to the "edge of the cliff."[15] General Mohammad Ali Jafari, the commander of Iran's Revolutionary Guards, has similarly described the postelection period as a "greater danger for the system and the Islamic Revolution" than the Iran-Iraq War. "We went to the brink of overthrow in this sedition," Jafari stated.[16] The regime's security services proved unreliable. Dissension spread even within the Guards. Khamenei had to dismiss several commanders. The ruling elite, which had

perfected the strategy of staging large pro-regime demonstrations, dared not bring its supporters out for more than six months.
Every commemoration day became an occasion for protest.

During Ahmadinejad's second term, Iran's ability to forge
a coherent approach to the nuclear talks was hobbled by internal divisions. Despite all the American denials, Khamenei
continued to blame the United States for his republic's internal
tremors and proved too suspicious of Obama's outreach to take
full advantage of the opportunities offered to him. The processes of diplomacy simply ground on. The P5+1 continued to
have inconclusive meetings with Iranian officials, who remained
intransigent and skeptical. Iran continued to advance its program, alarming both the Arab regimes and the Israeli state,
uneasy about what the Iranians were doing and what the
Americans were contemplating in terms of concessions.

The one facet of US policy that seemed to be working
beyond anyone's wildest expectations was the cumulative
impact of the sanctions. US Treasury officials, including Stuart
Levey, the key player behind the sanctions effort who had
stayed on for the first eighteen months of the Obama administration, continued to use Iran's truculence to great advantage
in terms of cutting off Iran from the global financial markets.
The massive repression and human rights violations taking
place in Iran even provoked the Europeans to join the sanctions
regime after the Obama administration succeeded in securing
an additional Security Council resolution condemning Iran's
continued nuclear activities. In the meantime, Congress passed
a series of devastating sanctions bills over Obama's objections
that eventually targeted the Islamic Republic's Central Bank.

For all practical purposes, Iran ceased to be a member of the global economy as it had fewer customers for its oil and was not able to process the oil payments that it did receive. By 2013, Iran's economy was crippled, offering the Obama White House unprecedented leverage that it soon began to squander.

In 2013, the election of Hassan Rouhani to succeed Ahmadinejad presaged a more clever approach to dealing with the twin mandates of the Iranian regime: reviving the economy and ensuring the success of the nuclear program. Rouhani's most effective ploy was to play the internal factional politics of Iran as a means of extracting concessions from the West. The American disposition to try to "help" Rouhani succeed ignored how Iran's internal politics had changed. In the aftermath of the 2009 convulsions, the Islamic Republic would no longer tolerate reformist politicians in its midst and had purged itself of all elements who sought a more accountable government. The Guardian Council systematically eliminated all candidates who might mount a challenge to the dominance of the existing regime. The days of reformists like former president Mohammad Khatami were over. Rouhani had always been a stalwart supporter of the clerical regime who advanced tactical arguments designed to win concessions on sanctions from the West. Rouhani and his suave foreign minister, Muhammad Javad Zarif, nonetheless convinced their American counterparts that they were moderates struggling against the hardliners precisely at a time when such demarcations no longer conditioned Iranian politics. The message from Tehran was that the only manner by which the pragmatists could salvage their position was for the West to support them. It was a message that was well received by the newly reelected Obama, who no longer felt the pressures of domestic politics as he charted radical departures from the traditional patterns of American policy and what he called the "Washington playbook" of the foreign policy establishment that his minions frequently derided as "the Blob."

Enchanted by Rouhani and the prospect of ensuring a pragmatic consolidation of power in Iran, the Obama administration eagerly sought an agreement to end the nuclear standoff. Officials from both sides began secretly meeting in Oman, and a nuclear negotiating process that had been conceived as a multilateral affair was increasingly reduced to bilateral haggling between the United States and Iran, with a multilateral fig leaf provided by the P5+1. The task at hand for the Obama team was not to secure a stringent arms control accord but to ensure that Rouhani and his allies maintained their power. Thus, the focus was less on the content of the agreement and more on an agreement for its own sake, one that would serve as a legacy foreign policy achievement for Obama as well as an agreement that would affect Iran's domestic political alignments.

After two years of painstaking diplomacy, the Obama administration finally concluded a nuclear agreement, the Joint Comprehensive Plan of Action. A close reading of the JCPOA reveals that it conceded an enrichment capacity that was too large, sunset clauses that were too short, and enforcement mechanisms that were too suspect to provide any real guarantee that Iran was abandoning its nuclear ambitions. Prior to the agreement, the United States had insisted that, given Iran's practical needs, it should only have a symbolic program of a few hundred centrifuges. Furthermore, the Islamic Republic could not be considered a member of the NPT in good standing until it secured the trust and confidence of the international community in the peaceful nature of its program, in particular by accounting for its past militarization activities. These were not just American aspirations but also the formal positions of the P5 + 1.

These prudent parameters were overtaken during the lengthy negotiations by the Obama administration's cavalcade of concessions. The administration soon brandished the notion that the real metric of success was establishing a minimal one-year breakout period that would allow Iran to maintain a substantial enrichment apparatus, in effect abandoning the goal of preventing development of an Iranian nuclear capability in favor of managing its emergence. The much-heralded one-year breakout period would only shrink over time as the JCPOA conceded that Iran can begin phasing out its primitive centrifuges in favor of more advanced ones. Even more troublesome is the agreement's stipulation that, after its limits expire, the "Iranian nuclear program will be treated in the same manner as that of any non-nuclear weapon state party to the NPT."[17] This means that Iran can proceed with the construction of an industrial-size nuclear infrastructure similar to that of Japan or any other member in good standing with the NPT. In that period, Iran could easily sprint to the bomb without risking timely detection. Even Obama admitted that once the time limits of the agreement had run their course, Iran would be "days" away from having a nuclear weapons capability.

One of the most disturbing aspects of the JCPOA was that once it had entered into force, it rescued Iran's economy. The clever handiwork of the Treasury officials that had effectively separated Iran from the global financial institutions was cast away. For all practical purposes, Iran is no longer a sanctioned country. The Europeans were back buying its oil, the Asian states were increasing their purchases, and international firms involved in areas as diverse as telecommunications and the airline industry were seeking new deals. Rouhani delivered on his promise of sustaining the essential features of the nuclear program while removing the barriers to Iran's economic recovery—although many Iranians complained that Iran was not benefiting sufficiently from the formal lifting of sanctions and sought even more efforts by the United States to help Iran get access to sources of investment and international financing, a demand that Secretary of State John Kerry was only too happy to try to meet during the last year of the Obama administration.

The JCPOA was indeed a landmark agreement, for it upended five decades of US nonproliferation and counterproliferation policy. It had long been the objective of both Republican and Democratic administrations to prevent the spread of dangerous nuclear technologies. Washington had sought to prevent both allies and adversaries from developing advanced enrichment capabilities. By contrast, the JCPOA conceded to an adversarial regime not only an enrichment capacity, but one that is likely to grow over time. Khamenei made no secret of Iran's aspiration to operate more than one hundred thousand centrifuges and trumpeted the JCPOA's apparent acquiescence in this objective. In effect, this would have been like Washington aiding the Soviet Union in constructing an atomic bomb in the 1940s or helping China develop its nuclear weapons capabilities in the 1960s. The Obama White House concluded an agreement that envisions a radical regime gaining access to a sophisticated nuclear infrastructure that will not permanently be limited to peaceful exploitation of atomic power.

Viewing the JCPOA and its permissive provisions as a great diplomatic achievement that "stopped the Iranian nuclear program without firing a shot," as its proponents argue, is only possible if one buys into the notion that once Iran is integrated into the global economy and recognized as a leading regional power it will become a responsible stakeholder. This was certainly the view of Obama, Kerry, and their various aides and flacks. This argument can only be given credence if one ignores the revolutionary dimensions of Iran's international policies that have proven remarkably durable over the past three decades. Those policies continue to sow chaos and disruption in a troubled and disordered Middle East, from Syria to Yemen to Bahrain.

LESSONS TO LEARN

The first lesson to learn from this lengthy experience is that Iran should be treated as a unitary nation-state and not a coterie of factions that American policy can manipulate to its advantage. The entire notion of factionalism must be reconsidered in the aftermath of the 2009 revolt, when the theocratic state purged the reformers in its midst. It is too facile to suggest that Iran has arrived at perfect internal consensus, but the divisions and rivalries that once polarized the clerical state are less urgent and less acute today. On core issues of regional hegemony and nuclear empowerment, the decision-making institutions of the Islamic Republic have reached a modus vivendi: Supreme Leader Ali Khamenei and President Hassan Rouhani share the same objectives, even though their tactics may at times differ.

Moreover, factionalism should never be used as a justification for absolving the Islamic Republic of responsibility for its domestic human rights transgressions or its violations of international law. The Carter administration was averse to adopting forceful measures against the hostage-takers for fear of undermining the "moderate" forces in the Iranian regime. The Reagan team's entire justification for participating in an unsavory arms-for-hostages deal was to empower the "moderate" Iranians who were seemingly poised to assume power after the Islamic Republic's founder, Ayatollah Khomeini, died. And no president has been more concerned about shifting Iranian politics in a pragmatic direction than Obama. By agreeing to a deficient arms control agreement and a lifting of sanctions, he and his advisors hoped to help Rouhani consolidate his power. Rouhani's Islamic Republic has gone on to wreak havoc in Iraq and Syria, destabilize the Persian Gulf region, and engage in massive repression of its citizens.

The second lesson to learn is that Iran is susceptible to threats of the use of force. During the hostage crisis, when there was much talk in Tehran about putting the diplomats on trial, Carter secretly warned Iran of possible retaliation if it proceeded with such steps. All talk of trials soon ceased. And it was the Carter officials themselves who were trying to induce Iran into ending the hostage crisis by intimating that should Reagan be elected, he might approach the issue entirely differently. The use of the "Reagan card" by the Carter White House was instrumental in ending the crisis. The Islamic Republic proved amenable when threatened, while it remained largely defiant when Carter was offering to set up tribunals that looked into America's historic misdeeds against Iran. A similar dynamic was at work when, after the Khobar Towers bombing in Saudi Arabia in which Iranian officials were complicit, the Clinton administration made clear that there were limits to its patience with Iranian-sponsored terrorism. Once again the regime pulled in its horns. In dealing with clerical oligarchs, threats work but blandishments usually don't.

The George W. Bush administration was a case study of what worked and what did not when it came to dealing with Iran. America's momentary success in displacing the Taliban regime and Saddam Hussein so unsettled the clerical regime that it quickly suspended its nuclear weapons program. Bush's denunciation of states that sponsor terrorism and pursue weapons of mass destruction was well noted in Tehran. And yet, the administration did not learn the lessons of its own success. During its second term, Secretary of State Rice sought talks with Iran on the nuclear issue while America's ambassador to Baghdad, Ryan Crocker, similarly wanted to engage Iran on means of stabilizing Iraq. Iran's response was to accelerate its nuclear activities and assault American forces in Iraq through its Shiite militia proxies.

Finally, for much of the last four decades, American presidents have hoped that offers of dialogue and the possibility of resumed relations could entice Iran into moderation. Carter wanted to settle the hostage crisis in a manner that did not foreclose the possibility of reestablishing relations with Iran. Bud McFarlane arrived in Tehran hoping to discuss ways of improving relations. And Obama spoke often of putting the contentious history of the two nations behind and moving to a better future with Iran. The point that they all missed is that Iranian officialdom sees a resumed relationship with the United States as an existential threat. Khamenei has persistently stressed that America now seeks regime-change not by invading countries but through commerce and cultural penetration. The point that many American presidents and pundits miss is that the Islamic Republic is a revolutionary state whose entire identity is invested in its hostility toward the West.

Toward a New Iran Strategy

IRAN HAS PLAYED A BIGGER PART IN THE ELABORATION OF American grand strategy in the postwar era than most Americans are aware of or are inclined to believe. Ever since the United States took on a larger global role at the end of World War II, its policy toward Iran has been characteristic of its larger strategic approach to the world. And Iran's involvement in US strategic calculations has also had important consequences for the country's political, economic, and social development. Today, the United States seems to be approaching another inflection point where a new approach to Iran will be necessary as part of a larger effort to combat the raging disorder in the Middle East. Before we examine that prospect, it would be worthwhile to see how the strategic interaction between the two countries has both shaped and reflected larger global strategic trends and the impact it has had on Iran's emergence as a major revisionist power in the broader Middle East.

US GRAND STRATEGY AND IRAN, 1945–2017

For most of its history, the United States has sought to avoid "permanent" or "entangling alliances." Even after its decisive entry into World War I, it did not become an "ally" but was rather, in President Woodrow Wilson's terms, "an associated power." By the time World War II had come to an end, however, the vast majority of the US national security elite had reached the conclusion that standing aloof from political commitments in Europe and Asia and a role as an "off-shore balancer" was not sustainable in the twentieth century. The traditional strategy of "continentalism" and defense of the Western Hemisphere was deficient, since it might well require periodic, massive military efforts to prevent Europe or Asia from being dominated by a hostile power. It would also be far more expensive than a strategy of preparedness. The latter would seek to aggregate the geopolitical weight of like-minded states into a "preponderance of power" that relied on a posture of forward defense, which would enable the rapid projection of US military force into key regions of the world that might come under threat from a hostile Soviet Union bent on extending its dominion.

During World War II, US national security planners and President Franklin D. Roosevelt initially hoped that the wartime alliance with the Soviet Union could be maintained and that a concert of great powers would sustain global peace, perhaps through a collective security mechanism like the United Nations. American hopes for a consensual world, with the great powers working in concert to promote peace and prosperity, dissipated as a series of crises undermined the notion that the Soviet Union would play its assigned role. This forced the United States to participate more actively in, and indeed to lead the formation of, new alliances in Europe, Asia, and the Middle East. While Europe continued to be foremost in the minds of most US policy-makers, Asia and the Middle East took on much greater importance than they had previously for the United States.

In broad terms, the United States found that the "threats which originated around the borders of the Atlantic and Pacific Oceans had been eliminated . . . only . . . to be replaced by a more serious threat originating in the heart of the Eurasian continent." As political scientist Samuel Huntington noted more than fifty years ago, the United States ultimately responded to this challenge through "the development of a system of alliances and the continuing application of American power through the maintenance of United States forces on the continent," with a navy whose purpose was "to utilize its command of the sea to achieve supremacy on land." The formalized commitments to defend allies were also useful for signaling to the Soviet Union in the new bipolar world. As Huntington observed, "Military alliances were one means of communicating American intentions to respond to the uses of force by other powers." In addition to access for US forces and facilities and signaling intent, the integrated military structure of the alliance provided for the aggregation of some military capabilities; facilitated the creation of a "free world" bloc whose security underpinned the economic recovery of Western Europe and Japan and denied their territory or industrial potential to the

Soviet Union; helped prevent the proliferation of nuclear weapons by providing extended nuclear deterrence to allies; assisted in attenuating the historical antagonisms that had divided allies by promoting multilateral ties; and provided a legitimating function for military operations. From the military perspective, the United States also became the framework nation for the formation of military coalitions and, through requirements for standards and interoperability, helped drive military modernization efforts around the world.[18]

US grand strategy in the Harry S. Truman era was motivated less by fear of a Soviet military invasion than by the perception that the United States needed to maintain a balance of power in Europe and Asia to avoid the kinds of conflicts that had erupted into World Wars I and II. The United States' real concern was "about postwar social, economic and political conditions in Western Europe and the occupied parts of Germany and Japan. The strategy of containment emerged from this postwar crucible." As historian Melvyn Leffler has written, "Gradually, a strategy emerged not simply for containing Soviet power, but also, eventually, for winning the Cold War."[19]

The successful integration of the core areas of Europe and Northeast Asia into an American-led security order depended on developments in the "undeveloped periphery." As Leffler has written, "Just as Western Europe depended on access to the petroleum of the Middle East and the natural resources of former and current colonial possessions in Asia and Africa, so, too, did Japan's rehabilitation depend on supplanting its former ties with Manchuria, North China, and Korea with new markets and raw materials in Southeast Asia." Iran's relations with the Soviet Union and Anglo-American allies had a lot to do with the souring of relations between the United States and Russia at the end of World War II. For the moment, the Near East remained a responsibility of the British. But over time, the United States would assume larger responsibilities in the region, and time and again Iran would play a role in that process as well.[20]

Britain had established a predominant position in Iran early in the twentieth century, driven in no small part by seeking a secure source of petroleum to fuel its naval forces. Occupied by the Allies during World War II, Iran became a vital transit route for Lend-Lease aid to the Soviet Union and played a crucial role in keeping the Red Army supplied, especially with logistical and transportation assistance. The deployment of thirty thousand US troops testified to the importance that the United States attached to this mission, as they commandeered Iranian ports, railheads, and roads to create an irreplaceable land route to supply the Soviet Union. Although Moscow repeatedly complained about the Anglo-American failure to open a second front in Europe, US assistance via the Persian corridor was a significant factor in keeping Russia in the war and maintaining its ability to defeat the German army on the Eastern Front. The United States also helped Iran by establishing a mission under Arthur Millspaugh, an advisor to the State Department's Office of Foreign Trade, to provide professional administration of public finances, a military aid mission to the army, and yet another effort under Colonel Norman Schwarzkopf (father of the future commander of the US Central Command) to reorganize the rural police, or gendarmerie.

This US assistance played out against a backdrop of Anglo-Soviet occupation of Iran.

For the United States, Iran provided an opportunity for the great powers to work in concert and not allow their competition for resources to disturb their alliance. Since the enfeebled state of the Iranian government threatened to provide an excuse for the continued intervention of Britain and Russia after the war, and since such a development could only aggravate the traditional rivalry of the two powers in Iran, State Department official John Jernegan argued that "disinterested American advisers" (whom Iran had already requested) and economic aid could "build up Iran to the point at which it will stand in need of neither British nor Russian assistance to maintain order in its own house." Therefore, "no peace conference could even consider a proposal to institute a Russian or British protectorate or recognize the predominance of Russian or British interests."[21]

Franklin Roosevelt himself told his secretary of state after the Tehran Conference in 1943 that he "was rather thrilled with the idea of using Iran as an example of what we do by an unselfish American policy." Then assistant secretary of state Dean Acheson regarded Roosevelt's ambition as "messianic globaloney." But the truth is that, throughout the Cold War, Iran tended to be emblematic of the overall approach that successive American presidential administrations took to US grand strategy and national security policy.[22]

The Tripartite Treaty called for the occupation to end within six months of the cessation of hostilities. As the war came to an end, the United States withdrew most, but not all, of its troops from Iran. By late 1945 and early 1946, the Soviet Union had not withdrawn its forces from northern Iran and alarm bells went off in Washington. The alarms were ringing in the context of Iran, specifically, but also about Soviet international behavior more broadly. Russian policies began to appear consistent with existing concerns that US policy-makers had about Soviet interest in the area from the Eastern Mediterranean through the Black Sea to the Near East. This was an area that appeared to be a focus of Soviet interest, as revealed in captured documents outlining the prewar Molotov-Ribbentrop negotiations that delineated German and Soviet spheres of interest. It also appeared to be consistent with the received wisdom that Imperial Russia had been seeking warm-water ports since at least the time of Catherine the Great.

In many discussions of the Iran crisis of 1946, as in other episodes, there is a tendency to deny any agency to the Iranian side and to see the Iranians as victims of machinations by predatory outside powers. In reality, from 1945 to 1946, the role of Iranian players—Prime Minister Ahmad Qavam, as well as others—was considerable. The Iranians sought to maximize their own power and Iran's freedom to maneuver against its big neighbor to the north, an outside imperial power that was suspect, and its new friend (and rising power) from afar that might be able to act as a buffer between the two countries that had occupied Iran during the war.

The shah, prime ministers Ebrahim Hakimi and Qavam, and other Iranian officials had plenty on their plates. In addition to the machinations of the great powers, they had ethnic and tribal groups to conciliate and leftist political forces with which to contend. In November 1945, Azeri separatists in the Soviet-occupied zone took advantage of local unrest, with much Soviet encouragement, to loosen Tehran's control over the northwest of the country. There were similar disturbances in Iranian Kurdistan. The central government's efforts to dispatch military forces to quash the strife were met by Soviet military forces at Qazvin, ninety miles outside Tehran, although the Iranian government may have exaggerated the size and scope of Soviet military activity to influence the American audience. As the March 1946 deadline for Soviet withdrawal approached, the Iranians formally complained to the United Nations Security Council. As the crisis intensified during the summer and fall of 1946, US policy-makers, including Truman aide Clark Clifford, viewed the Soviet refusal to let the Iranian government reinforce Tabriz as a violation of the Allied commitment to the independence of Iran that was agreed to at the Tehran Conference in 1943. Against a backdrop of obstreperous behavior by the Soviets in the meetings of foreign ministers aimed at developing a peace treaty for Europe, the apparent encroachments in the Middle East were a matter of grave concern. As Clifford noted, these moves were weakening the US and British positions in the region and "our continued access to oil in the Middle East is especially threatened by Soviet penetration into Iran." One month later the Joint Chiefs of Staff reinforced that conclusion, noting:

As a source of supply (oil) Iran is an area of major strategic interest of the United States. From the standpoint of defensive purposes the area offers opportunities to conduct delaying operations and/or operations to protect United States-controlled oil resources in Saudi Arabia. In order to continue any military capability for preventing a Soviet attack overrunning the whole Middle East including the Suez–Cairo Area, in the first rush, it is essential that there be maintained the maximum cushion of distance and difficult terrain features in the path of possible Soviet advances launched from the Caucasus–Caspian area. Otherwise the entire Middle East might be overrun before sufficient defensive forces could be interposed. As to counter-offensive operations, the proximity of important Soviet industries makes the importance of holding the Eastern Mediterranean–Middle Eastern area obvious. This is one of the few favorable areas for counter-offensive action. Quite aside from military counter-offensive action in the area, the oil resources of Iran and the Near and Middle East are very important and may be vital to decisive counter-offensive action from any area.

From an afterthought before World War II, Iran had become a central consideration as the United States began to develop a global strategy to contain Soviet power. In the face of this challenge, the United States supported Iran at the United Nations and called for Soviet withdrawal. With a nuclear monopoly, US policy-makers believed they were in a strong position. Although it is not clear that an actual ultimatum was issued, when the Soviets withdrew, Truman and his colleagues believed they had faced down Russia in the first confrontation of the emerging Cold War.[23]

The complex crisis in Iran was rooted in Iranian politics and society. But Russian actions elsewhere in Europe, and especially

Turkey, convinced US officials that Moscow increasingly represented a threat to global order and would only respond to robust diplomacy backed by the threat of force. Iran became the catalyst for more active US engagement on the periphery of Eurasia and the first testing ground of this "get tough" policy with the Soviets. In 1947, the Iranians rejected the Soviet bid for Iranian oil, but almost immediately began pressing the British for a larger share of the proceeds from the sale of Iranian oil by the Anglo-Iranian Oil Company. This largely commercial dispute took on far greater geopolitical significance in the context of a global confrontation with communism that became much more menacing after the Chinese intervention in the Korean War in 1950.

The United States faced two challenges: (1) the Anglo-Iranian conflict over oil and (2) providing some guarantee that the solicitude the United States had shown for Iran's security in 1946 would continue in the troubling circumstances of a globalized Cold War with the Soviet Union. In the wake of the outbreak of the Korean War, the Truman administration answered this problem by working to facilitate a negotiated settlement of Anglo-Iranian differences in the petroleum sector (while preserving US interests) and undertaking a large conventional and nuclear military buildup in keeping with the foundational National Security Council strategy document, NSC-68. The problem, however, proved to be intractable. As the Truman administration came to an end, US policy-makers began to consider other options.

In 1953, when Dwight Eisenhower succeeded Truman, he, along with Secretary of State John Foster Dulles and his brother

Allen Dulles, who was director of the Central Intelligence Agency, developed a different, more asymmetric approach to the Soviet strategic challenge. Fearful that the large Truman-era buildup would bankrupt the US economy—defense spending under Truman rocketed up to 13 percent of GDP—Ike and the Dulles brothers combined a reliance on nuclear deterrence, or "massive retaliation," and covert action by intelligence operatives to hold the Soviet Union at bay and roll back any encroachments on the periphery of the free world. Much as Iran had been the test case for the Truman administration's "get tough" policy with the Soviets in the early years after World War II, it became the precedent for the Eisenhower team's reliance on clandestine activity in combating perceived Soviet gains in the emerging Third World.

In Iran, a crisis arose from the efforts of Prime Minister Mohammad Mossadeq, a nationalist politician, who had long sought to reclaim Iran's oil industry from Britain's control. The British, whose naval predominance in the early twentieth century had been tied to access to Persian oil, saw the issue simultaneously in economic, strategic, and prestige terms. When Truman's efforts to mediate proved unavailing—largely but not solely due to Mossadeq's intransigence and political miscalculations—the long-running crisis entered a more perilous phase. With the Iranian economy grinding to a halt as the result of a Western embargo on Iranian oil sales, Mossadeq's government encountered significant dissent at home. The prime minister dealt with the opposition with an increasingly authoritarian bent, seeking expanded and emergency powers in constitutionally dubious ways. Soon, his base of support, notably including the Iranian clergy, began to unravel, raising fears at home and abroad that the communist Tudeh Party would likely be the beneficiary of a government collapse. The young shah and Mossadeq now embarked on a labyrinthine game of move and countermove that ultimately led to a "countercoup" that, with US and British covert support, led to the prime minister's removal from office and the reestablishment of the shah as the predominant political player in Iran. This was largely the result of an internal Iranian political dynamic at play. But over time, the myth that American and British spies had imposed the shah on the Iranian people took root and continues to haunt the strategic interaction of the two countries to this day.

As the drama in Tehran played out, the United States began to subtly edge the British aside as the shah's and Iran's primary international partner and patron. Iran, as a result, began to loom larger in Washington's designs for regional security in the Middle East, for which the United States was taking on increasing responsibility in the 1950s. The early Cold War conception envisioned an Anglo-American partnership, with the British as the senior partner, in a Middle Eastern Command or Middle East Defense Organization, based on the ongoing relationship between Britain and Egypt. This would leverage the United Kingdom's bases there to contain Soviet expansionism into the Middle East and serve as the forward point of departure for an air atomic attack on the Soviet Union if war broke out. As the politics of a British presence at the large Suez base became more problematic, the Americans abandoned the initial concept in favor of a turn toward "alliance reinforcement" among the "outer ring countries" of the "northern tier," where the early Cold War clashes involving Turkey and Iran had played out. Britain invited Turkey and Iran, along with Iraq and Pakistan, to join the Baghdad Pact in 1955. As one scholar noted, "The Baghdad Pact—later the Central Treaty Organization (CENTO)—was conceived by the Western powers as an instrument of cold-war containment, to supersede failed US attempts to build a Middle East Defence Organization." It collapsed with the departure of Iraq after the 1958 coup in that country. As Henry Kissinger has noted, from the outset the Baghdad Pact lacked a common purpose, shared threat perceptions, and the "capacity to pool strengths." It was, in short, an empty vessel.[24]

The Kennedy administration brought a different sensibility to the Cold War in general, and the Middle East in particular. The administration's policy-makers, all believers in the New Frontier proclaimed by John F. Kennedy, sensed that Eisenhower's reliance on the threat of nuclear war was not credible and that the older Eisenhower had presided over Soviet gains in the Third World. In particular, the members of Kennedy's team were preoccupied by Soviet Premier Nikita Khrushchev's declaration of support for "wars of national liberation" in the decolonized nations of the world. Moreover, they believed that the United States was failing to meet the Soviet challenge by tying itself to stodgy, old-guard regimes that lacked a strategy for modernizing their countries and putting them on the path to economic "takeoff" and growth, according to the stages of economic development identified by New Frontiersman and future national security advisor Walt Whitman Rostow. Iran, although distinctly not a priority for Kennedy and his team, nonetheless became a bit of a testing ground for the emphasis on modernization and reform in Kennedy's national security strategy.

During Kennedy's Vienna summit meeting with Khrushchev in June 1961, the Soviet premier taunted his younger American counterpart by noting that Iran, a client state of the United States, was governed by a reactionary regime. The president replied that if the shah resisted efforts to reform, change would come in any event. The shah, for his part, was anxious to maintain the economic growth that had characterized the 1950s as well as US patronage among the great powers. After an initial push for political reform in Iran was met with both bureaucratic resistance in the United States and reluctance on the part of the shah, the Iranian government embarked on a policy of economic development that included a significant element of land reform. Dubbed the White Revolution by the shah, it seemed to propitiate the desire for economic and social reform that the Kennedy administration had embraced. But it also carried fateful consequences for Iran. Agrarian reforms put the shah's regime at odds with important elements of the clergy, who were significant landholders. Other elements of the shah's program—privatization of state factories, women's suffrage, and intensified efforts at eliminating illiteracy in rural areas—also brought the regime into conflict with the clergy. One particularly vocal critic was Ruhollah Khomeini, whose aversion to the White Revolution coincided with his opposition to the increasing US role in providing military assistance to Iran. Khomeini was exiled in 1963 to neighboring Iraq and eventually Paris, where he continued to agitate against the shah for the next fifteen years.

The American passion for modernization brought about unintended results in other parts of the world in the 1960s, notably Vietnam, where the United States embarked on a nation-building exercise in support of the government of Ngo Dinh Diem with the objective of preventing South Vietnam from coming under the control of the communist North. By the end of the decade, the United States was embroiled in an endless guerrilla war against a wily local enemy, with seemingly no prospect of a satisfactory outcome. At the same time, while the United States was strategically distracted by the disaster in Southeast Asia, Britain, which largely had responsibility for the security order in the Persian Gulf states, was forced to withdraw from there after a defense review found that the United Kingdom could not afford to fund both European security and the country's obligations "east of Suez." The British decided to prioritize European defense.

The British withdrawal from east of Suez, along with the 1967 Six-Day War between Israel and its Arab neighbors, transformed US security policy in the Middle East. The US Navy was now patrolling the Persian Gulf and increasingly saw the Middle East as an area of vital US interest. At the same time, pressures to reduce US global involvement as a consequence of the Vietnam War weighed heavily on US policymakers. Richard Nixon was elected in 1968, in part to end US involvement in Vietnam and to develop a post-Vietnam strategy for US national security. Early in his term, Nixon did articulate a new strategy that put the onus on American allies and partners to bear a greater share in providing for their own defense. Some powers would be essentially "deputized" to provide regional security, while the United States supplied arms, equipment, and training as well as the benefit of an implicit US security guarantee. The Nixon doctrine paved the way for a significant increase in US military aid to allies in the Middle East, specifically the Kingdom of Saudi Arabia and Iran, which had already been characterized during the Lyndon Johnson administration as the "twin pillars" of regional stability. The United States focused its energies on building up local militaries. Total arms transfers from the United States to Iran alone increased over 500 percent from 1970 to 1972 and sales to Saudi Arabia increased twentyfold in the same period. Over the next decade, the United States committed $22 billion in arms sales to Iran and $35 billion to Saudi Arabia. Both countries became increasingly dependent on American security assurances and competed for preeminence in the region by rapidly expanding their respective militaries.

The dynamics of the US relationship with these Middle East client states shifted after the 1973 Arab oil embargo, which was a direct response to American support for Israel during the Yom Kippur War. The use of oil as an economic and political weapon underscored the vulnerability of the United States and its allies to supply shortages and price hikes. The tripling of world oil prices dealt an especially painful blow to Europe's economy and boosted skyrocketing inflation. The embargo and contemporaneous nationalization of oil and gas resources drastically changed the terms of the relationship between the US government and regional powers, but that shift did not prevent

American government and companies from developing new ties with Middle Eastern regimes. The new petrodollar windfall flowing into Middle Eastern coffers was largely reinvested in the West, providing new linkages between the United States and leaders in Saudi Arabia, Kuwait, Iran, and other Gulf countries. The windfall also provided the means to finance growing arms sales to the region from the United States and other Western powers. Around this time the Nixon administration began to slightly favor the Iranians over the Saudis. In response to increased Soviet patronage of the "revolutionary" regime in Iraq, and due to the shah's long-standing efforts to make Iran the preeminent power of the Gulf, the administration provided a blank check to the shah, allowing him to buy weapons that were not available to other customers. Whether or not unrestricted arms sales and the use of Iran as a proxy was a wise policy, it was a source of controversy at the time and remains a matter of contentious debate to this day. Many scholars believe that the heavy investment by Iran in military hardware distorted the development of the Iranian economy, which in turn provided grist for Khomeini's critique and helped pave the way for the 1978–79 revolution.

The Iranian revolution was the first indicator of the rise of Islamic fundamentalism, a phenomenon Laurence Freedman has called the second wave of postcolonial radicalism—the first wave consisting of Nasserist pan-Arab nationalism—and the first of several incidents in 1979 that marked a new era of upheaval in the Middle East. In late 1979, Iranian students seized a large group of US diplomats and held them hostage for more than a year. A few weeks later, the Kingdom of Saudi Arabia was severely shaken when Wahhabi extremists seized the Grand Mosque in Mecca. A Shiite revolt in the oil-rich Al-Hasa region of the country broke out the following month. The instability in Saudi Arabia illustrated that extremist Islam was not a uniquely Shiite phenomenon limited to Iran, but one that could spread throughout the Arabian Peninsula. Moreover, the almost-simultaneous sacking of the US embassy in Islamabad, Pakistan, carried out spontaneously by crowds that blamed the United States for the attack on the Grand Mosque, demonstrated the ability of false ideas to travel quickly in the emerging information age. The Soviet invasion of Afghanistan in December 1979 injected a dimension of great-power politics into the region's simmering brew of conflict and strengthened US security relationships with Middle Eastern countries that feared a Soviet drive into the Persian Gulf.

The cumulative effect of the momentous events of 1979 and 1980 forced the United States to articulate clearly its interests in the Persian Gulf region and publicly declare its willingness to use military force to protect them. Although the United States continued to rely on local allies to preserve regional order and access to its energy resources, Washington reorganized and equipped its forces to intervene rapidly if necessary to safeguard US interests. This included increased access to facilities and the prepositioning of equipment in the region. The necessity for a rapid intervention capability was underscored in 1980 by the failed effort to rescue US hostages held in Tehran. Iran's role in America's grand strategic calculations moved from that of ally to a source of terrorism and proliferation of weapons of mass destruction—two issues that increasingly preoccupied

American policy-makers as the Cold War wound down and gave way to an era of unipolar US predominance.

In his 1980 State of the Union address, President Carter declared, "Let our position be absolutely clear: An attempt by any outside force to gain control of the Persian Gulf region will be regarded as an assault on the vital interests of the United States of America, and such an assault will be repelled by any means necessary, including military force." Although Carter's emphasis was on the unacceptability of any outside power controlling the vital Persian Gulf waterways, it became increasingly clear that the United States would not tolerate the domination of those waters by a hostile local power—either Iran or Iraq—as well. Washington continued to encourage and oversee the modernization of the Saudi military and enhance cooperation between the other Gulf states, now organized in the Gulf Cooperation Council. But the Carter doctrine's broader strategic vision for the region signaled a new era of direct US military intervention in the Persian Gulf.[25]

As the conflicts in the region simmered, another one surfaced. An increasingly aggressive Iraq with aspirations for regional dominance took advantage of the hostage crisis and Tehran's provocations to launch the Iran-Iraq War in late 1980. Some observers have suggested that the Carter administration had given a "green light" to Baghdad. Now that scholars have access to captured Iraqi records, it is clear that such speculation is totally unwarranted. In fact, before the hostage crisis, American officials did warn Iran that Iraq may have been getting ready to attack. Both the embassy and CIA functionaries shared intelligence with the Iranian government, hoping to avert a war. All these warnings were ignored by the provisional government that was itself soon cast aside by Khomeini.

Although the war was primarily a brutal land conflict between Iran and Iraq, it represented a serious threat to shipping via the Persian Gulf and hence attracted disproportionate attention from the international community because of its potential impact on energy markets. These concerns came to a head in the late 1980s as a result of the so-called Tanker War. In order to protect Kuwaiti and other shipping through the Gulf, the United States led an international effort to "reflag" much of the shipping and convoy it safely through the choke points of the Gulf. Tensions escalated after an antiship mine hit the USS *Samuel B. Roberts* in April 1988. In retaliation, the US Navy undertook its largest engagement since the end of World War II, Operation Praying Mantis, which led to the sinking of half of the Iranian navy and substantial damage to a number of Iranian oil platforms.

The war devastated both Iraq and Iran and the "war of the cities" highlighted the dangers of ballistic missile proliferation. But the domestic Iranian narrative of the Islamic Republic as a beleaguered underdog that was persecuted by the West and its Sunni Arab neighbors reinforced the grievances that had fueled the revolution in 1979 and gave the regime enduring legitimacy for many of those in the generation of Iranians who lead the country today. This helps to explain the lingering, deep anti-Americanism and suspicion toward the West that persist today among the clerical elite and the generation of war veterans who populate the senior reaches of the regime.

In the wake of the Gulf War, the United States abandoned the effort to maintain a balance of power between Iran and Iraq, developing a strategy of dual containment to blunt the danger to US interests and regional stability. Iran was a revolutionary state that continued to support terrorism, violently opposed the Arab-Israeli peace process through its proxy Hezbollah, egregiously abused human rights, and appeared to be pursuing development of the nuclear fuel cycle, raising the specter of nuclear proliferation. The Saddam regime in Iraq brutally repressed its Kurdish and Shiite populations and continued to nurse its ambitions for nuclear weapons and regional hegemony.

The new US policy toward the region, announced in May 1993 by National Security Council official Martin Indyk, stated:

> The Clinton Administration's policy of "dual containment" of Iraq and Iran derives in the first instance from an assessment that the current Iraqi and Iranian regimes are both hostile to American interests in the region. Accordingly, we do not accept the argument that we should continue the old balance of power game, building up one to balance the other. We reject that approach not only because its bankruptcy was demonstrated in Iraq's invasion of Kuwait. We reject it because of a clear-headed assessment of the antagonism that both regimes harbor towards the United States and its allies in the region. And we reject it because we don't need to rely on one to balance the other.[26]

Although dual containment had some success in checking Iraq, efforts to maintain sanctions on Iraq and inspections of its weapons of mass destruction program became increasingly politically costly for the Clinton White House as international support began to wane over time. Iran, for its part, continued to withstand a range of sanctions imposed by Congress. Dual containment was not as successful as it might have been, since US unilateral sanctions did not lead to parallel efforts by US partners and allies. As one scholar has noted, "While the United States sought the containment of both states, in effect it pursued two separate policies simultaneously—a fact that became more obvious as Clinton, in his second term, sought to mend fences with Iran while Washington's attitude toward Saddam Hussein's Iraq remained consistently hostile."[27] This effort, however, coexisted uneasily with increased concerns about the construction in Iran by Russia of a nuclear power reactor at Bushehr, which raised questions about Iran's potential interest in access to the full nuclear fuel cycle and continued support for terrorism abroad, including the Khobar Towers bombing in Saudi Arabia. A lengthy FBI investigation into the latter, headed by Director Louis Freeh, turned up evidence of involvement at the highest levels of the Iranian regime.

In the aftermath of the 9/11 tragedies, the Bush administration undertook the ambitious task of reforming the political culture of the Middle East. The invasion of Iraq was intended to usher in democracy that would soon spread to other corners of the Middle East. In this sense, the Bush White House overestimated its capabilities and underestimated the region's stubborn political order, as well as the manner in which its many ethnic and religious divisions would devour Washington's noble aspirations.

As we have seen, America's entrapment in Iraq's civil war greatly benefited the Islamic Republic. A charter member of the "axis of evil" was still the leading sponsor of terrorism, while once more resuming its nuclear activities. The need to stabilize Iran's simmering nuclear program led the administration to cast aside any regime-change aspirations it may have had and enter into talks with the mullahs. The negotiations proved inconclusive, but—much to its credit—the administration did not fundamentally redraw its red lines. In the meantime, the elimination of two of Iran's most enduring rivals—Saddam's regime in Iraq and the Taliban in Afghanistan—paved the way for the projection of its power in places once thought of as unimaginable by Tehran. As Bush left the White House, Iran had not just survived America's shock-and-awe campaign, but was putting together the building blocks of a sophisticated nuclear infrastructure. Tehran's nuclear aspirations excited concerns not just in the United States but throughout the region and in Europe as well. After the Bush administration came to an end, press reports began to surface of a sophisticated campaign to sabotage the Iranian program using a computer virus that was referred to as Stuxnet in the various published accounts. Like Agatha Christie's *Murder on the Orient Express*, in this instance there were so many potential suspects that the provenance of the virus was difficult to establish.[28]

Barack Obama came into office with the expansive ambition of reconciling with America's enemies and drawing down the US presence in the Middle East. Both of these objectives required reconciliation with Iran's truculent clerics. The Islamic Republic had no use for Obama's transformational diplomacy and his attempts at better relations, but it did take advantage of his gullibility to obtain an agreement that ensured Iran's path to the bomb. In the meantime, America's withdrawal from Iraq and its indifference to Syria led to further surges of Iranian power. All this seemed acceptable to Obama, who continuously called on US allies to share the Middle East with Iran.

Donald Trump has inherited from his predecessor a Middle East where Iran holds a commanding position across the region. He is also saddled with an arms control agreement that does little to obstruct Iran's nuclear ambitions. How he attempts to deal with all this will determine whether he will succeed or fail in the region.

NEW WINE IN OLD BOTTLES

The Islamic Republic may be at an impasse. An ideological experiment born in a century that saw so many radical postulations has managed to crawl into this one. Today, the theocratic state relies on a combination of patronage and coercion to sustain its power. It no longer possesses an ideology that convinces its citizens, who seem to use every commemorative occasion to register a protest against its rule. And yet, for the Islamic Republic to be displaced by a democratic regime, America has to embark on an active and aggressive policy. The great advantage that Washington has in this confrontation is the clerical state's many mistakes.

The faded history of the Cold War tends to focus little on Soviet Premier Alexei Kosygin. In the mid-1960s, Kosygin pressed for economic reforms that involved loosening state controls. This was, in effect, the precursor for the China model that Deng Xiaoping embraced in the late 1970s. Kosygin's effort to inject an element of enterprise into the Soviet economy was rejected by an aging Politburo led by Leonid Brezhnev. The Soviet Union chose instead to rely on oil wealth, which seemed like a smart decision amid the price hikes that followed the Arab oil embargo in the early 1970s. But once oil markets went from boom to bust, the Kremlin had a problem it could neither mitigate nor resolve. Failure to sustain the Kosygin reforms, which would have been cushioned by rising state revenues, meant that Mikhail Gorbachev's belated effort to reform the Soviet economy in the 1980s had no chance of succeeding.

Beyond its unwise command economy and failures of reform, the Soviet Union also made some costly foreign policy decisions in the 1970s that exacerbated its economic vulnerabilities. The Kremlin began investing money and resources in areas peripheral to core Soviet security concerns, such as Africa and Latin America. Eventually, those imperial impulses led Moscow to the invasion of Afghanistan, a disastrous decision that further bled Russia. A combination of economic mismanagement and imperial misadventures significantly contributed to the Soviet Union's demise.

The Soviet Union's past uncannily resembles the Islamic Republic's present and, one must hope, its future. President Rouhani is celebrated in the West for his pragmatic approach to state planning and international relations. But viewed from another angle, he is making a series of mistakes that could imperil the state he is seeking to revive. There is scant evidence that he intends to embark on the structural changes necessary to resolve Iran's mounting economic problems. Inflation and unemployment plague Iran, while rampant corruption remains unaddressed. Like Russia's former communist leaders, Rouhani appears to hope that sanctions relief, access to global financial markets, and ramped-up oil sales will prove sufficient. Ironically, it is Iran's reactionary supreme leader, Ali Khamenei, who is actively calling for the development of local industries and markets, as opposed to the sort of short-term remedies that appear attractive to Iran's president and his supposedly modernist aides.

Like the Soviet Union of the 1970s, Iran has embarked on an imperial mission whose costs are more obvious than its benefits. The billions that Iran spends to sustain Bashar al-Assad in Syria and the lavish sums it invests in terrorist organizations such as Hezbollah may offer regional sway, but they further burden the Islamic Republic's depleted economy. No policy has been more destructive to Iran's practical interests than its unrelenting hostility toward Israel. The two states have neither territory in dispute nor a long history of animosity, yet an ideologically driven Islamic Republic has made assaulting the Jewish state one of its principal obsessions. This has led Iran to partner with unsavory actors, alienate much of the international community, and distress a public that has no stake in the Israeli-Palestinian conflict.

Still, in Iran's miscalculations lies an opportunity for the United States to deal effectively with one of its most entrenched adversaries. The task at hand is to use all of America's coercive tools to press for genuine change in Iran.

CONTAINMENT BEGINS AT HOME

The task of American diplomacy is similar to the one that Reagan faced with the Soviet Union: not just renegotiating a better arms control agreement but devising a comprehensive policy that undermines the theocratic regime. In this regard, there is nothing as powerful as the presidential bully pulpit. Reagan's denunciations of communist rule did much to galvanize the opposition and undermine the Soviet empire. Dissidents in jail and others laboring under the Soviet system took heart from an American president who championed their cause. Obama chose the opposite course and remained silent as protesters in 2009 called on America to support their cause. His administration paid scant attention to Iran's human rights abuses.

The uprisings in late 2017 once more surprised the United States. Suddenly Iranians took to the streets in more than eighty cities, protesting their economic plight and calling for the overthrow of the regime. The Trump administration did not seem as flat-footed as its predecessor and quickly embraced the cause of the demonstrators. All national protest movements leave in their wake nascent organizations and new leaders, and it is Washington's task now to find ways to support and sustain these forces of dissent.

Given the Islamic Republic's cruelty and corruption, the opposition spans the entire social spectrum. Iranian citizens have given up not just on the Islamic Republic, but even on religious observance, as mosques go empty during most Shiite commemorations. Three decades of theocratic rule have transformed the Iranian people into arguably the most secular population in the Muslim world. The middle class and the working poor are equally hard-pressed by the regime's incompetence and corruption. Even the senior ayatollahs are beginning to realize the toll that entanglement with politics has taken on Shiite Islam. America has ready allies in Iran and must make an effort to empower those who share its values.

Economic sanctions are a critical aspect of any policy of pressuring the Islamic Republic. The experience of the past few years has shown that the United States has a real capacity to shrink Iran's economy and bring it to the brink of collapse. The fewer resources the regime has at its disposal, the less capable it is of sustaining a cadre whose loyalty is largely purchased with subsidies, its ideological commitment having greatly eroded. The guardians of the revolution are well aware of the unreliability of their coercive services—the government had difficulty repressing the Green Movement and seemed reluctant to dispatch its conscripts to shoot down working class protests in December 2017. Once deprived of money, the mullahs will find it difficult to fund the patronage networks that are essential to their rule at home and their imperial adventures abroad.

PUSHING BACK IN THE REGION

An equally important dimension of undermining the Iranian regime is to shrink its imperial footprint. So as it stresses Iran's economy and divides its society, the United States should also push back against its influence in the Middle East. By contesting Iran's gains, Washington can impose additional costs on the regime and contribute to regional stability. Iran's leaders believe that the vitality of their revolution mandates its export. And it is that export that must be jeopardized as a means of undermining the revolution.

The best arena in which to push back on Iran is the Persian Gulf region. The Gulf sheikhdoms, led by Saudi Arabia, are already locked into a region-wide rivalry with Iran. The Sunni states have taken it upon themselves to contest Iran's gains in the Gulf and the Levant. Washington should not only buttress these efforts but press all Arab states to embark on a serious attempt to reduce their commercial and diplomatic ties to Tehran. The price of American guardianship is for Sunni Arab states to do their part in resisting the rising Shiite power of Iran.

Getting the Gulf states to take common action has always been difficult. The United States should help the Gulf states, not only as they battle Iranian proxies in Syria, Iraq, and Yemen, but also as they deal with a range of other challenges. These include protecting themselves against Iran's efforts to undermine their internal security, defending their economic infrastructure (such as oil and gas platforms, water-desalination plants, and tourist sites), and preventing Iran from interdicting their energy exports along key transit routes.

Even in a disorderly Middle East there are opportunities to forge constructive new alliances. The enmity that Saudi Arabia and Israel share toward Iran should be the basis for bringing these two countries closer together. Instead of lecturing the Saudis to share the Middle East with Iran and hectoring Israelis about settlements, the United States should focus on imaginative ways of institutionalizing the nascent cooperation that is already taking place between Riyadh and Jerusalem. The United States should press both countries to move beyond intelligence-sharing and perhaps forge complementary trade ties, with Saudi oil exchanged for Israeli technological products. History rarely offers opportunities to realign the politics of the Middle East. A truculent Iran has presented this chance.

Another alliance that needs refurbishing after years of neglect and rancor is the US-Israeli relationship. One of the most spurious, yet pervasive, arguments has been that America's ties with Israel damage its standing in the Middle East. To be effective in the Middle East, it is claimed, Washington should put some distance between itself and the only democracy in the region. Any strategy of pushing back on Iran has to have Israel as one of its core elements. The Islamic Republic respects Israeli power and fears its integration in the Middle East. An Israel even more closely tied to the United States enhances our deterrent power. And an Israel that is mending fences with Sunni Arab states only empowers the anti-Iran alliance and further isolates the Iranian theocracy in the region. America's task should not be to distance itself from Israel, but to bring all elements of its anti-Iran coalition together.

Iraq may seem like a protectorate of Iran today, but this is a condition that most Iraqi leaders want to escape. Iraq was once the seat of Arab civilization and the center of the region's politics. Iraqis understand that Iran has exercised a pernicious influence in their country and that Iranian-sponsored Shiite militias have been responsible for atrocities in places like Tikrit that further accentuate the country's sectarian divides. Iraq cannot be whole and free so long as Iran interferes in its affairs. A commitment by the United States to once more rehabilitate the Iraqi army and bureaucracy can go a long way toward ending its ties to Tehran. No Iraqi Arab wants to be subordinate to imperious Shiite Persians. Once Iraq frees itself of Iranian dominance, it may yet find a path back to the Arab world and once more serve as a barrier to Iranian power.

At a practical level, Washington should also push Baghdad to govern more inclusively, so that the central government is seen as benefiting Sunnis and Kurds and not just the Shiites. It should make an outreach to the Sunni tribes on a scale equivalent to what took place during the 2007 surge of US troops. And it should ramp up its military assistance to Kurds and the Sunni tribal forces, intensify the air campaign against the Islamic State in both Iraq and Syria, and embed US personnel in the Iraqi military at lower levels than it currently does. A heightened US presence in Iraq need not entail a massive combat force there, but it would mean a larger troop presence and thus a greater risk of casualties. Again, the price for greater US involvement should be a commitment on the part of local actors to press back against Tehran and its enablers.

The tragedy of Syria is that, as the Obama administration stood aloof and preoccupied itself with useless international summits, Iran and Russia possibly succeeded in saving the Assad dynasty. It is important to stress that Syria cannot be rehabilitated so long as Bashar al-Assad remains in power. For both strategic and humanitarian reasons, we should embrace this task. Pushing back on Iran means harassing its Syrian proxy. At the very least, as the opposition strengthens, Iran will have to face the dilemma of sinking more resources and men into a quagmire or cutting its losses, just as the Soviet Union was forced to do in Afghanistan.

A regime as dangerous to US interests as the Islamic Republic requires a comprehensive strategy to counter it. This means exploiting all of Iran's vulnerabilities, increasing the costs of its foreign adventures, weakening its economy, and supporting its domestic discontents. Pursuing that strategy will take time, but it will eventually put the United States in a position to impose terms on Iran. We should not settle for an arms control agreement that paves the way for an Iranian bomb, but rather a restrictive accord that ends its nuclear weapons aspirations. We should seek to compel Iran to cease its regional subversion, not create power vacuums that encourage it. And we should move human rights up the agenda, not look the other way as Iran's leaders oppress their people.

The Middle East is a region that is constantly dividing against itself. During the Cold War, it was polarized with radical republics seeking to undermine the traditional monarchies.

The forces of Arab nationalism led by Egypt and then Iraq were challenging the legitimacy and longevity of the conservative order. The United States entered this contested terrain, actively took sides, and buttressed its allies' resistance. Today, the region is once more divided, this time along sectarian lines. A revisionist Iran and its Shiite allies are seeking to subvert the tattered foundations of the Arab state system. On the other side stand Saudi Arabia and the incumbent Sunni states with Israel lurking in the background. This is a contest for the future of the Middle East. And it is a contest that America cannot afford to lose. The United States stood aside during the Obama years, with calamitous consequences. The Trump administration would be wise to reject such reticence and embrace Ronald Reagan's slogan on dealing with the Soviet Union: we win, they lose.

NOTES

1. For Gates's observation on the search for moderates, see the transcript of his remarks at the Carnegie Endowment for International Peace, "Nuclear Weapons and Deterrence in the 21st Century," October 28, 2008, accessed January 2, 2018, http://carnegieendowment.org/files/1028_transcrip_gates_checked.pdf.

2. Hassan Rouhani, *National Security and Nuclear Diplomacy* (Tehran: Center for Strategic Research, 2013), 69–70.

3. Islamic Republic News Agency (IRNA), April 2, 2005.

4. Muhammad-Reza Mahdavi-Kani, *Khatarat-i Ayatollah Mahdavi-Kani* (Tehran, 2007), 219.

5. Warren Christopher, *American Hostages in Iran: The Conduct of a Crisis* (New Haven, CT: Yale University Press, 1985), 118.

6. Christopher, *American Hostages in Iran*.

7. Text of Algiers Accord, 1981.

8. Text of Algiers Accord, 1981.

9. US Congress, House of Representatives and Senate Select Committee to Investigate Covert Arms Transactions with Iran, *Report of the Congressional Committee Investigating the Iran-Contra Affair* (Washington, DC: Government Printing Office, 1987), 280.

10. Robert M. Gates, *Duty: Memoirs of a Secretary at War* (New York: Alfred A. Knopf, 2014), 336.

11. Burns made the statement to CNN. "Iran Arming Taliban, U.S. Claims," June 13, 2007, accessed January 17, 2018, http://www.cnn.com/2007/WORLD/asiapcf/06/13/iran.taliban/index.html.

12. Zalmay Khalilzad, *The Envoy: From Kabul to the White House, My Journey through a Turbulent World* (New York: St. Martin's Press, 2016), 164–165.

13. For the origins of Khomeini's slogan during the Iranian revolution, see John Limbert, *Negotiating with Iran: Wrestling the Ghosts of*

History (Washington, DC: United States Institute of Peace Press, 2009), 170.

14. "Text: Obama's Speech in Cairo," *New York Times*, June 4, 2009.

15. Misagh Parsa, *Democracy in Iran: Why It Failed and How It Might Succeed* (Cambridge, MA: Harvard University Press, 2016), 249.

16. Parsa, *Democracy in Iran,* 250.

17. Text of the Joint Comprehensive Plan of Action.

18. Samuel Huntington, "National Policy and the Transoceanic Navy," reprinted by US Naval Institute (blog), accessed January 19, 2018, https://blog.usni.org/posts/2009/03/09/from-our-archive-national-policy-and-the-transoceanic-navy-by-samuel-p-huntington.

19. Melvyn P. Leffler, "The Emergence of an American Grand Strategy, 1945–1952," in *The Cambridge History of the Cold War*, vol. 1, *Origins*, eds. Melvin P. Leffler and Odd Arne Westad (Cambridge, UK: Cambridge University Press, 2010), 74–77, 81.

20. Leffler, "Emergence of an American Grand Strategy," 82–83.

21. Eduard M. Mark, "Allied Relations in Iran, 1941–1947: The Origins of a Cold War Crisis," *Wisconsin Magazine of History* 59, no. 1 (Autumn 1975): 52.

22. The account in the previous two paragraphs draws on Mark, "Allied Relations in Iran, 1941–1947," 51–63; and Gary R. Hess, "The Iranian Crisis of 1945–46 and the Cold War," *Political Science Quarterly* 89, no. 1 (March 1974): 117–146.

23. Clifford is quoted in Richard Pfau, "Containment in Iran, 1946: The Shift to An Active Policy," *Diplomatic History* 1, no. 4 (October 1, 1977): 364–365; for the JCS memorandum, see Herbert A. Fine, John G. Reid, and John P. Glennon, *Foreign Relations of the United States, 1946, The Near East and Africa*, vol. 7, document 396 (Washington, DC: US Government Printing Office, 1969).

24. Louise Fawcett, "Alliances and Regionalism in the Middle East," in *International Relations of the Middle East*, ed. Louise Fawcett (New York: Oxford University Press, 2005), 183; Henry Kissinger, *Diplomacy* (New York: Simon and Schuster, 1994), 527.

25. For the text of Carter's speech, see "State of the Union," January 23, 1980, accessed January 17, 2018, http://www.presidency.ucsb.edu/ws/?pid=33079.

26. Martin Indyk "The Clinton Administration's Approach to the Middle East," Washington Institute for Near East Policy, conference report, Soref Symposium, May 1993.

27. Alex Edwards, *"Dual Containment" Policy in the Persian Gulf: The USA, Iran, and Iraq, 1991–2000* (New York: Palgrave Macmillan, 2014), 75.

28. James P. Farwell & Rafal Rohozinski, "Stuxnet and the Future of Cyber War," *Survival* 53, no. 1: 23–40.

SUGGESTIONS FOR FURTHER READING

Abrahamian, Ervand. *Iran between Two Revolutions*. Princeton, NJ: Princeton University Press, 1982.

———. *Khomeinism: Essays on the Islamic Republic*. London: I.B. Tauris, 1993.

———. *Tortured Confessions: Prisons and Public Recantations in Modern Iran*. Berkeley, CA: University of California Press, 1999.

Algar, Hamid. *The Roots of the Islamic Revolution*. London: Open Press, 1983.

Amanat, Abbas. *Iran: A Modern History*. New Haven, CT: Yale University Press, 2017.

Ansari, Ali M. "Iran and the US in the Shadow of 9/11: Persia and the Persian Question Revisited." *Iranian Studies* 39, no. 2 (June 2006): 155–70.

———. "The Myth of the White Revolution: Mohammad Reza Shah, 'Modernization' and the Consolidation of Power." *Middle Eastern Studies* 37, no. 3 (July 2001): 1–24.

Arjomand, Said Amir. *The Turban for the Crown: The Islamic Revolution in Iran*. Oxford: Oxford University Press, 1988.

Azimi, Fakhreddin. *The Quest for Democracy in Iran: A Century of Struggle against Authoritarian Rule*. Cambridge, MA: Harvard University Press, 2008.

Baker, Peter. *Days of Fire: Bush and Cheney in the White House*. New York: Doubleday, 2013.

Bakhash, Shaul. *The Reign of the Ayatollahs: Iran and the Islamic Revolution*. New York: Basic Books, 1984.

Bayandor, Darioush. *Iran and the CIA: The Fall of Mosaddeq Revisited*. New York: Palgrave Macmillan, 2010.

Bill, James A., and Wm. Roger Louis, eds. *Musaddiq, Iranian Nationalism, and Oil*. Austin, TX: University of Texas Press, 1988.

Binder, Leonard. *Iran: Political Development in a Changing Society.* Berkeley, CA: University of California Press, 1964.

Brands, Hal. "Before the Tilt: The Carter Administration Engages Saddam Hussein." *Diplomacy and Statecraft* 26, no. 1 (January 2015): 103–23.

———. "Saddam Hussein, the United States, and the Invasion of Iran: Was There a Green Light?" *Cold War History* 12, no. 2 (May 2012): 319–43.

Buchan, James. *Days of God: The Revolution in Iran and Its Consequences.* London: Simon & Schuster, 2013.

Bush, George W. *Decision Points.* New York: Crown Publishers, 2010.

Castiglioni, Claudia. "No Longer a Client, Not Yet a Partner: The US-Iranian Alliance in the Johnson Years." *Cold War History* 15, no. 4 (2015): 491–509.

Cheney, Dick, with Liz Cheney. *In My Time: A Personal and Political Memoir.* New York: Threshold Editions, 2011.

Cohen, Eliot, Eric S. Edelman, and Ray Takeyh. "Time to Get Tough on Tehran: Iran Policy After the Deal." *Foreign Affairs* 95, no. 1 (January/February 2016): 64–75.

Crist, David. *The Twilight War: The Secret History of America's Thirty-Year Conflict with Iran.* New York: Penguin Press, 2012.

Dobbins, James. *After the Taliban: Nation-Building in Afghanistan.* Washington, DC: Potomac Books, 2008.

Doenecke, Justus D. "Iran's Role in Cold War Revisionism." *Iranian Studies* 5, no. 2 (Spring–Summer 1972): 96–111.

———. "Revisionists, Oil and Cold War Diplomacy." *Iranian Studies* 3, no. 1 (Winter 1970): 23–33.

Edwards, Alex. *"Dual Containment" Policy in the Persian Gulf: The USA, Iran, and Iraq, 1991–2000.* New York: Palgrave Macmillan, 2014.

Elm, Mostafa. *Oil, Power, and Principle: Iran's Oil Nationalization and Its Aftermath.* Syracuse, NY: Syracuse University Press, 1992.

Eshraghi, F. "Anglo-Soviet Occupation of Iran in August 1941." *Middle Eastern Studies* 20, no. 1 (January 1984): 27–52.

———. "The Immediate Aftermath of Anglo-Soviet Occupation of Iran in August 1941." *Middle Eastern Studies* 20, no. 3 (July 1984): 324–51.

Fawcett, Louise. "Revisiting the Iranian Crisis of 1946: How Much More Do We Know?" *Iranian Studies* 47, no. 3 (2014): 379–99.

———. *Iran and the Cold War: The Azerbaijan Crisis of 1946*. New York: Cambridge University Press, 1992.

Fischer, Michael M. J. *Iran from Religious Dispute to Revolution*. Madison, WI: University of Wisconsin Press, 1980.

Freedman, Lawrence. *A Choice of Enemies: America Confronts the Middle East*. New York: Public Affairs, 2008.

Gasiorowski, Mark J. "The 1953 Coup D'etat in Iran." *International Journal of Middle East Studies* 19, no. 3 (August 1987): 261–86.

Gates, Robert M. *Duty: Memoirs of a Secretary at War*. New York: Alfred A. Knopf, 2014.

Gavin, Francis J. "Politics, Power, and U.S. Policy in Iran, 1950–1953." *Journal of Cold War Studies* 1, no. 1 (Winter 1999): 56–89.

Goode, James. "Reforming Iran during the Kennedy Years." *Diplomatic History* 15, no. 1 (January 1991): 13–29.

Gordon, Michael, and Bernard Trainor. *The Endgame: The Inside Story of the Struggle for Iraq, from George W. Bush to Barack Obama*. New York: Pantheon Books, 2012.

Heiss, Mary Ann. *Empire and Nationhood: The United States, Great Britain, and Iranian Oil, 1950–1954*. New York: Columbia University Press, 1997.

Hess, Gary R. "The Iranian Crisis of 1945–46 and the Cold War." *Political Science Quarterly* 89, no. 1 (March 1974): 117–46.

Jentleson, Bruce W. *With Friends like These: Reagan, Bush and Saddam, 1982–1990*. New York: W.W. Norton, 1994.

Johns, Andrew L. "The Johnson Administration, the Shah of Iran, and the Changing Pattern of U.S.-Iranian Relations, 1965–1967: 'Tired of Being Treated like a Schoolboy.'" *Journal of Cold War Studies* 9, no. 2 (Spring 2007): 64–94.

Kaussler, Bernd. "From Engagement to Containment: EU-Iran Relations and the Nuclear Programme, 1992–2011." *Journal of Balkan and Near Eastern Studies* 14, no. 1 (March 2012): 53–76.

Keddie, Nikki. *Modern Iran: Roots and Results of the Revolution*. New Haven, CT: Yale University Press, 2006.

Khalilzad, Zalmay. *The Envoy: From Kabul to the White House, My Journey through a Turbulent World*. New York: St. Martin's Press, 2016.

Kimball, Jeffrey. "The Nixon Doctrine: A Saga Of Misunderstanding." *Presidential Studies Quarterly* 36, no. 1 (March 2006): 59–74.

Kinzer, Stephen. *All the Shah's Men: An American Coup and the Roots of Middle East Terror.* Hoboken, NJ: John Wiley & Sons, 2003.

Kissinger, Henry. *White House Years.* Boston: Little, Brown and Co., 1979.

Kurzman, Charles. *The Unthinkable Revolution in Iran.* Cambridge, MA: Harvard University Press, 2004.

Leffler, Melvyn P. *A Preponderance of Power: National Security, the Truman Administration, and the Cold War.* Stanford: Stanford University Press, 1992.

Louis, Wm. Roger. "The British Withdrawal from the Gulf, 1967–1971." *Journal of Imperial and Commonwealth History* 31, no. 1 (January 2003): 83–108.

Lytle, Mark Hamilton. *The Origins of the American-Iranian Alliance, 1941–1953.* New York: Holmes & Meier, 1987.

Maloney, Suzanne. *Iran's Political Economy since the Revolution.* Cambridge: Cambridge University Press, 2015.

Mark, Eduard M. "Allied Relations in Iran, 1941–1947: The Origins of a Cold War Crisis." *Wisconsin Magazine of History* 59, no. 1 (Autumn 1975): 51–63.

———. "The War Scare of 1946 and Its Consequences." *Diplomatic History* 21, no. 3 (Summer 1997): 383–415.

Marsh, Steve. "Continuity and Change: Reinterpreting the Policies of the Truman and Eisenhower Administrations toward Iran, 1950–1954." *Journal of Cold War Studies* 7, no. 3 (Summer 2005): 79–123.

———. "The United States, Iran and Operation 'Ajax': Inverting Interpretive Orthodoxy." *Middle Eastern Studies* 39, no. 3 (July 2003): 1–38.

McFarland. Stephen L. "A Peripheral View of the Origins of the Cold War: The Crises in Iran, 1941–1947." *Diplomatic History* 4, no. 4 (Fall 1980): 333–51.

McGlinchey, Stephen. "Richard Nixon's Road to Tehran: The Making of the U.S.-Iran Arms Agreement of May 1972." *Diplomatic History* 37, no. 4 (September 2013): 841–60.

McGlinchey, Stephen, and Andrew Moran. "Beyond the Blank Cheque: Arming Iran during the Ford Administration." *Diplomacy and Statecraft* 27, no. 3 (2016): 523–44.

Menashri, David. *Post-Revolutionary Politics in Iran: Religion, Society and Power*. New York: Routledge Press, 2001.

Moslem, Mehdi. *Factional Politics in Post-Khomeini Iran*. Syracuse, NY: Syracuse University Press, 2002.

Mottahedeh, Roy. *The Mantle of the Prophet: Religion and Politics in Iran*. New York: Simon & Schuster, 1985.

Motter, T.H. Vail. *The Persian Corridor and Aid to Russia*. Washington, DC: Center of Military History, 1952.

Nemchenok, Victor V. "In Search of Stability Amid Chaos: US Policy toward Iran, 1961–1963." *Cold War History* 10, no. 3 (August 2010): 341–69.

Njølstad, Olav. "Shifting Priorities: The Persian Gulf in US Strategic Planning in the Carter Years." *Cold War History* 4, no. 3 (April 2004): 21–55.

Odom, William E. "The Cold War Origins of U.S. Central Command." *Journal of Cold War Studies* 8, no. 2 (2006): 52–82.

Palmer, Michael. *Guardians of the Gulf: A History of America's Expanding Role in the Persian Gulf, 1833–1992*. New York: The Free Press, 1992.

Parsa, Misagh. *Democracy in Iran: Why It Failed and How It Might Succeed*. Cambridge, MA: Harvard University Press, 2016.

Pfau, Richard. "Containment in Iran, 1946: The Shift to an Active Policy." *Diplomatic History* 1 no. 4 (Fall 1977): 359–72.

Pollack, Kenneth M. *The Persian Puzzle: The Conflict between Iran and America*. New York: Random House, 2004.

Popp, Roland. "An Application of Modernization Theory during the Cold War? The Case of Pahlavi Iran." *International History Review* 30, no. 1 (March 2008): 76–98.

Rice, Condoleezza. *No Higher Honor: A Memoir of My Years in Washington*. New York: Crown Publishers, 2011.

Roosevelt, Kermit. *Countercoup: The Struggle for the Control of Iran*. New York: McGraw-Hill, 1979.

Rumsfeld, Donald. *Known and Unknown: A Memoir.* New York: Sentinel, 2011.

Sanger, David. *The Inheritance: The World Obama Confronts and the Challenges to American Power.* New York: Harmony Books, 2009.

Sauer, Tom. *Coercive Diplomacy by the EU: The Case of Iran.* Discussion Papers in Diplomacy. The Hague: Netherlands Institute of International Relations "Clingendael," 2007.

Scott-Clark, Cathy, and Adrian Levy. *The Exile: The Stunning Inside Story of Osama bin Laden and Al Qaeda in Flight.* New York: Bloomsbury Publishing, 2017.

Solomon, Jay. *The Iran Wars: Spy Games, Bank Battles, and the Secret Deals that Reshaped the Middle East.* New York: Random House, 2016.

Takeyh, Ray. "The Myths of 1953." *Weekly Standard*, July 14, 2017.

————. "What Really Happened in Iran: The CIA, the Ouster of Mosaddeq, and the Restoration of the Shah." *Foreign Affairs* 93, no. 4 (July/August 2014): 2–12.

US National Commission on Terrorist Attacks upon the United States. *The 9/11 Commission Report: Final Report of the National Commission on Terrorist Attacks upon the United States.* Washington, DC: Government Printing Office, 2004.

Wilber, Donald. *Overthrow of Premier Mossadeq of Iran, November 1952–August 1953.* Clandestine Service History. Washington, DC: Central Intelligence Agency, 1969. Full text available online at National Security Archive Electronic Briefing Book No. 28, "The Secret CIA History of the Iran Coup, 1953," ed. Malcolm Byrne, November 29, 2000, accessed January 20, 2018, https://nsarchive2 .gwu.edu/NSAEBB/NSAEBB28.

Yegorova, Natalia I. *The "Iran Crisis" of 1945–46: A View from the Russian Archives.* Cold War International History Project Working Paper No. 15. Washington, DC: Woodrow Wilson International Center for Scholars, 1996.

Zonis, Marvin. *Majestic Failure: The Fall of the Shah.* Chicago: University of Chicago Press, 1991.

————. *The Political Elite of Iran.* Princeton, NJ: Princeton University Press, 1971.

ABOUT THE AUTHORS

Ambassador Eric S. Edelman is the Roger Hertog Distinguished Practitioner-in-Residence at the Philip Merrill Center for Strategic Studies at Johns Hopkins University–SAIS and Counselor at the Center for Strategic and Budgetary Assessments. Edelman retired as a career minister from the US Foreign Service in 2009. He has served in senior positions at the departments of State and Defense as well as at the White House, where he led organizations providing analysis, strategy, policy development, security services, trade advocacy, public outreach, citizen services, and congressional relations. He was undersecretary of defense for policy, DoD's senior policy official, from 2005–2009. He served as US ambassador to Finland in the Clinton administration and to Turkey in the George W. Bush administration (in which he also served as Vice President Dick Cheney's principal deputy assistant for national security affairs). He received a BA in history and government from Cornell University and a PhD in US diplomatic history from Yale University. Edelman was awarded the Order of the White Rose by the Government of Finland in 2009 and received the Legion d'Honneur from the Government of France in 2011. He now chairs the National Defense Strategy Commission appointed by Congress.

Ray Takeyh is Hasib J. Sabbagh Senior Fellow for Middle East Studies at the Council on Foreign Relations and previously served as a senior advisor on Iran at the State Department. He is the coauthor of *The Pragmatic Superpower: Winning the Cold War in the Middle East* (W. W. Norton, 2016) and is the author of three previous books, *Guardians of the Revolution: Iran and the World in the Age of the Ayatollahs* (Oxford University Press, 2009), *Hidden Iran: Paradox and Power in the Islamic Republic* (Henry Holt, 2006), and *The Origins of the Eisenhower Doctrine: The US, Britain, and Nasser's Egypt, 1953–1957* (St. Martin's Press, 2000). He has also written more than 250 articles and opinion pieces in many news outlets including *Foreign Affairs*, the *New York Times*, the *Wall Street Journal*, and the *Washington Post*.

HERBERT AND JANE DWIGHT
WORKING GROUP ON
ISLAMISM AND THE
INTERNATIONAL ORDER

THE HERBERT AND JANE DWIGHT WORKING GROUP ON ISLAMISM AND THE INTERNATIONAL ORDER seeks to engage in the task of reversing Islamic radicalism through reforming and strengthening the legitimate role of the state across the entire Muslim world. Efforts draw on the intellectual resources of an array of scholars and practitioners from within the United States and abroad, to foster the pursuit of modernity, human flourishing, and the rule of law and reason in Islamic lands—developments that are critical to the very order of the international system.

Founded by Fouad Ajami, the Working Group is cochaired by Hoover fellows Russell A. Berman and Charles Hill. Recent contributors include Mokhtar Awad, Tony Badran, Fabrice Balanche, Hal Brands, Cole Bunzel, Harel Chorev, Colin Dueck, Kassem Eid, Joseph Felter, Reuel Marc Gerecht, Bernard Haykel, Kelly A. Hammond, Michael Wahid Hanna, Emile Hokayem, Qutaiba Idlbi, David S. Maxwell, Abbas Milani, Afshin Molavi, Camille Pecastaing, Itamar Rabinovich, Karim Sadjadpour, Robert Satloff, Patricia Sloane-White, Shaun Tan, Samuel Tadros, Eric Trager, Sanam Vakil, Meredith L. Weiss and Paul Wolfowitz.

HERBERT AND JANE DWIGHT WORKING GROUP
ON ISLAMISM AND THE INTERNATIONAL ORDER

Many of the writings associated with this Working Group
are published by the Hoover Institution Press.
Materials published to date are listed below.

BOOKS

Freedom or Terror: Europe Faces Jihad
Russell A. Berman

The Myth of the Great Satan: A New Look at America's Relations with Iran
Abbas Milani

Torn Country: Turkey between Secularism and Islamism
Zeyno Baran

Islamic Extremism and the War of Ideas: Lessons from Indonesia
John Hughes

The End of Modern History in the Middle East
Bernard Lewis

The Wave: Man, God, and the Ballot Box in the Middle East
Reuel Marc Gerecht

Trial of a Thousand Years: World Order and Islamism
Charles Hill

Jihad in the Arabian Sea
Camille Pecastaing

The Syrian Rebellion
Fouad Ajami

Motherland Lost: The Egyptian and Coptic Quest for Modernity
Samuel Tadros

Iraq after America: Strongmen, Sectarians, Resistance
Joel Rayburn

In this Arab Time: The Pursuit of Deliverance
Fouad Ajami

America and the Future of War: The Past as Prologue
Williamson Murray

Israel Facing a New Middle East: In Search of a National Security Strategy
Itamar Rabinovich and Itai Brun

Russia and Its Islamic World: From the Mongol Conquest to the Syrian Military Intervention
Robert Service

INDEX